Parent Letters for the Intermediate Grades

Adapted from *The Learning Letter*, Morton Malkofsky Publishing
Editor: Karen P. Hall
Illustrator: Catherine Yuh
Project Director: Carolea Williams

Table of Contents

Introduction

Parent Letters for the Intermediate Grades is designed to strengthen the home-school connection and reinforce learning at home. The letters offer parents meaningful parent/child activities in the core subject areas of reading, language arts, math, science, and social studies.

A *Did You Know?* section is included at the top of each letter to explain why an activity is important and provide background in the activity's subject area. Sections are written in easy-to-understand language, free from educational jargon.

A *How You Can Help* section explains each parent/child activity. Activities are designed as a fun way to support what is being taught in school.

Reproducibles follow specific activities throughout the book. Send each reproducible home with its corresponding parent letter.

When working with parent letters, consider the following suggestions.

- Use activities that support currently-taught units. With simultaneous home/school learning, students receive the reinforcement they need to make ideas "stick."

- Send letters home on brightly-colored paper so they will be noticed. Inform parents of the color so they can watch for them.

- Provide a parent letter support system. Invite parents to call or write when they have questions about an activity.

- During the first week of school, send home the Welcome Back letter and an activity letter as homework. (If children feel the first one is required, they will be more likely to try it, like it, and beg for more!)

- Send home a group of letters just before vacation as an activity packet.

- Write your own letters to reinforce ideas specific to your curriculum. Keep them with this book for reuse.

- Laminate previously-sent letters and keep them in a central location. Check the letters out so students can repeat favorites again and again.

Dear Parents,

Welcome to a new school year! Your child is about to embark on an exciting learning adventure—and you can come along! Throughout the year, you will receive letters that provide important information and fun activities to help your child with reading, language arts, math, science, and social studies.

You can recognize these letters by their format. There is a *Did You Know?* section that offers an explanation of why the activity is important and background in the activity's subject area. The second section is called *How You Can Help*. This section explains a parent/child activity through clear, easy-to-follow directions.

Try each activity as you receive it. If you don't have time to do an activity right away, keep the letter for later use. Activities are designed to be used by you and your child, but many can be completed as a family.

You may wish to keep the letters in a three-ring binder. That way, you can invite your child to choose favorite or new activities to do during vacation or after the school year ends.

Try one activity and you'll try them all. They're quick, easy, and best of all, an opportunity to spend special time with your child.

Sincerely,

Parent Letters for the Intermediate Grades © 1997 Creative Teaching Press

Dear Parents,

Did You Know?

Your child can become a better student by becoming a better "homeworker." Homework offers important reviewing and learning time away from the classroom, helping your child become a more independent learner. To help your child get the most from homework, try the following tips—your child may actually start looking forward to it!

How You Can Help

1. Help your child find a special quiet place to study. It may be the bedroom, basement, or attic—it doesn't matter where, as long as he or she will not be disturbed.

2. Provide your child with materials he or she needs to complete the work, such as paper, pencils, pens, crayons, markers, or other special supplies.

3. Set a schedule. Have your child work for 30 minutes a day whether homework is assigned or not. A routine will become a habit. (If no homework is assigned, have your child read or work on an art project for 30 minutes.)

4. Show your child samples of his or her neatest work. Explain that homework should meet this neatness standard.

5. When your child has trouble, help him or her without giving answers. Instead, give clues such as *Reread the third sentence to find the answer. The question asks for the total. Does that mean the numbers all together or only the number left over?*

6. Help your child think like a teacher. When doing assignments, have your child ask him- or herself, *What should students remember? What are the most important ideas and facts? What are the steps needed to solve this problem?*

7. When studying for a test, show your child how to create a "fake test" with questions and answers written just like the teacher's. Do the test with your child.

8. For spelling tests, have your child create flash cards each week. Invite your child to quiz you as well as be quizzed.

Parent Letters for the Intermediate Grades ©1997 Creative Teaching Press

Dear Parents,

It's been a great year, and I hope these letters have been a big part of the success.

Letter activities can be used again and again—so pull them out over vacation. Try these suggestions to make vacation activities more meaningful.

- Invite your child to choose activities, whether old favorites or new ones.

- To keep activities interesting, vary subject area each day. For example, do a reading activity on Monday, science on Tuesday, math on Wednesday, language arts on Thursday, and social studies on Friday.

- After each activity, go to the library and challenge your child to discover more about the activity's subject.

- Have an activity day. Invite several of your child's friends to participate in a day of letter-activity fun.

- Get the whole family involved—complete activities together.

Have a wonderful vacation!

Sincerely,

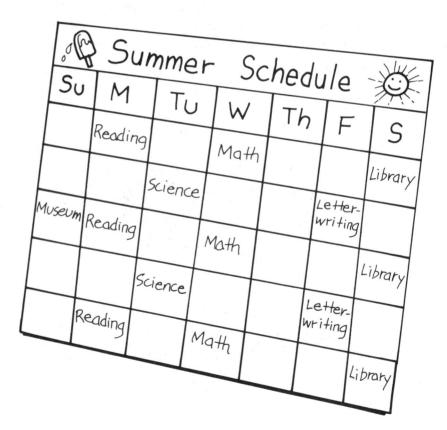

Parent Letters for the Intermediate Grades ©1997 Creative Teaching Press

Dear Parents,

Did You Know?

Children are more motivated to read when they personally relate to book characters and associate story events to real-life experiences. If you want your child to be intrigued by written words, read aloud stories involving favorite hobbies, true-life mysteries, natural wonders, or any other topic your child finds fascinating. The following activity is one way to put "meaning into reading," making it an enjoyable experience for the whole family.

How You Can Help

1. On clear, starry nights, take your family outside for shared reading. Spread out a blanket or comfortable cushions to sit on. For extra motivation and excitement, pitch a tent to create a camping environment while reading aloud.

2. Take turns reading aloud stories about different constellations. Have your child search the sky to see how many constellations he or she can find.

3. Discuss what it would be like to be an astronaut and travel among the stars. Read stories about voyages in outer space. Invite your child to close his or her eyes, or stare up into the stars as you read stories aloud.

4. Encourage your child to write his or her own stories about constellations and space travel. Invite him or her to read the stories aloud at the next "camp out."

Dear Parents,

Did You Know?

Shared reading builds self-esteem. Children feel appreciated and accepted knowing their thoughts and ideas are listened to and appreciated by others. Help your child grow up to be a confident, self-assured adult by reading together on a regular basis, giving him or her your undivided attention and words of encouragement. Get the whole family involved to make the experiences even more meaningful and rewarding.

How You Can Help

1. Invite each family member to cut out his or her favorite choice for funniest, scariest, or most unusual newspaper or magazine story.

2. Have family members read their articles aloud at the dinner table.

3. Take a vote to decide whose article is the best.

4. Post the winning article on a bulletin board or the refrigerator.

5. Add new "winners" every week.

6. Encourage your child to visit your local library to find winning articles in old newspapers and magazines.

7. As a variation, have family members copy a favorite line from a book they're reading and post it for all to enjoy.

Parent Letters for the Intermediate Grades ©1997 Creative Teaching Press

Dear Parents,

Did You Know?

Books on tape are not only fun, they are great reading motivators and skill builders. Children who are hesitant to read on their own will enjoy these "talking books." By listening to tape-recorded stories, your child will increase his or her vocabulary, improve oral reading fluency, and become a more "dramatic" storyteller. Books on tape will be a big hit with your child, especially if they're homemade.

How You Can Help

1. Tape-record a favorite book. Use dramatic voices for different characters and add sound effects for extra fun.

2. Invite your child to listen to the recorded story during meals, before bedtime, or during family trips.

3. Stop the recording periodically to discuss and predict story plot. Have your child identify where the story takes place, describe the main characters, and summarize what has happened so far.

4. Have your child listen to recorded stories more than once. Encourage him or her to follow along in the book while listening to the tape.

5. Invite your child to make his or her own "talking books." Encourage him or her to tape and listen to "practice runs" before making the final version.

6. Invite your child to give the recorded stories as gifts to family members and friends.

Dear Parents,

Did You Know?

Encouraging children to "preview and practice" improves reading fluency. Children benefit from going over words in their heads before sharing them aloud. If you've ever read a speech "cold turkey," then you know the importance of preparing in advance. Use the following activity to help your child read more clearly, smoothly, and confidently.

How You Can Help

1. Before having your child read aloud, have him or her silently read through the story. Encourage your child to mouth the words while reading.

2. Model reading aloud to your child. First have him or her listen to you read in a dull, boring tone—be sure to pause, repeat, and mumble words every so often. Invite your child to give you pointers on how to improve.

3. Read the same passage again, this time clearly, smoothly, and with "feeling." Have your child listen to and compare the two versions.

4. Switch roles and have your child read aloud. Have your child tape-record and listen to him- or herself read. Ask your child to self-assess how clearly each word is spoken, how smoothly he or she reads from one sentence to the next, and how "captivating" it is to listen to the recording.

5. Encourage your child to practice reading into a tape recorder and listening to the tape until he or she is satisfied with the results.

6. Discuss how facial expressions and body language make spoken words "come alive." Read aloud and model the behavior for your child.

7. Videotape your child reading aloud twice. The first time, have him or her stand still and read without emotions or feeling. The second time, ask your child to read more dramatically. Invite your child to view each version and compare results.

There stood a huge brown bear.

Parent Letters for the Intermediate Grades ©1997 Creative Teaching Press

Dear Parents,

Did You Know?

Children who read for pleasure become better readers. The next time your child reads a comic book, the Sunday funnies, or even the ingredients off a cereal box, encourage it—the practice alone will improve overall reading skills. Booster recreational reading by inviting your child to select his or her own reading materials and to read for pleasure before bedtime. The next time your child has a sleep-over, try the following party theme as a "novel" way to promote the joys of reading.

How You Can Help

1. Suggest that your child invite friends to a slumber party where everyone brings a favorite book to share.

2. Have children read aloud in pairs and dramatize favorite parts of the stories.

3. Award special party favors such as bookmarks, comics books, mystery novels, or joke books to those who read the funniest, strangest, scariest, or saddest passages.

4. Invite party-goers to play Book Charades by pantomiming favorite book titles and characters for others to identify.

5. As a special treat, help your child prepare and serve party foods that tie in to popular books. For example, have your child read aloud Tomie dePaola's *Popcorn Book,* then serve yummy popcorn for friends to enjoy.

Reading Aloud

Dear Parents,

Did You Know?

When you make shared reading a "family tradition," you help strengthen reading and oral-language skills. When children read aloud and discuss stories with family members, they improve their ability to draw conclusions about what they've read, communicate facts and ideas more clearly, expand their use of vocabulary, and learn from what others say. Use the following activity to learn more about families around the world as you and yours enjoy special reading time together.

How You Can Help

1. Invite each family member to select a short story, fable, fairy tale, or poem written in another country.

2. Take turns reading literature selections aloud. Invite family members to guess each story's country of origin.

3. Compare different writing styles used in the stories. Discuss similarities and differences in the characters, setting, vocabulary, and the overall "lessons" or "morals" in the stories.

4. Place a world map on the wall and use sticky notes to place the title of each book in the appropriate country.

5. Collect and share travel brochures for places mentioned in the stories.

6. Encourage your child to read additional literature, such as international magazines and newspapers, to learn more about countries around the world.

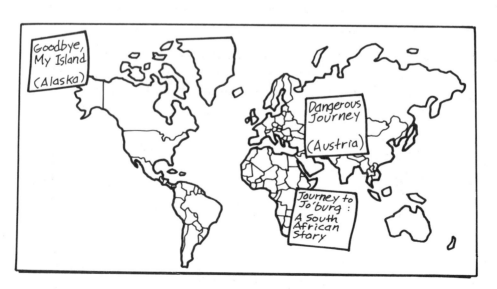

Parent Letters for the Intermediate Grades © 1997 Creative Teaching Press

Dear Parents,

Did You Know?

Critiquing a television show is similar to analyzing the plot of a good book. They both involve a main story line, characters faced with difficult decisions, and a moral or lesson. By taking time to examine and discuss television programs with your child, you can change passive, "mindless" viewing into active, educational experiences.

How You Can Help

1. While watching a television show with your child, talk about events that unravel in the story. Take time during commercial breaks to analyze what has occurred and predict what will happen next.

2. Invite your child to "talk back" to the TV—cheer, boo, and express agreement or disagreement with a character's actions.

3. Have your child compare real family life to that portrayed on TV. Encourage him or her to identify similarities and differences between television families and your own.

4. Discuss how television friends act toward each other compared to those in real life. Take time to discuss the meaning of true friendship.

5. After watching a program with your child, have him or her jot down each major event of the plot on separate index cards. Mix up the cards and have your child arrange them in correct sequence.

6. For extra challenge and fun, turn off the volume while watching a show and have your child write down what he or she thinks is being said. Videotape the show so your child can compare notes with the actual conversations.

7. Point out the similarities between evaluating a television show and analyzing the plot of a book. Explain that all stories, whether on film or in print, involve a similar progression of actions and events. Encourage your child to voice thoughts and opinions about storybook characters and their actions whenever you read aloud.

Reading Comprehension

Dear Parents,

Did You Know?

Newspapers are "all-in-one" readers for both adults and children. Whatever your child's interests, newspapers have it all—sports, famous personalities, science, world affairs, books, bargains, food, and entertainment. Even though newspapers are written for adults, there are many ways they can be used to strengthen your child's reading skills. Try some of the following "just-for-fun" activities to encourage your child to pick up, explore, and enjoy newspapers.

How You Can Help

1. Introduce the paper to your child by encouraging him or her to simply browse through the pages. Invite your child to share what captures his or her eye.

2. Have your child glance at headlines, look at pictures, and skim through captions before settling down to more serious reading. Invite him or her to predict what each story is about by using picture, caption, and headline "clues."

3. Head for the funnies to enjoy shared reading with your child. Invite him or her to read the part of one comic strip character while you read the other. Encourage your child to "act" the role as he or she reads aloud.

4. Motivate your child to read independently by giving a "sneak peak" of a story. Give a brief overview of an article, highlighting the more exciting parts without giving away the ending.

5. Encourage your child to "help you read" by reading the first part of a news story, then asking him or her to finish reading it aloud for you.

6. Invite your child to give you "updates" of an ongoing news piece such as a political race, a sports competition, or a storm watch.

Parent Letters for the Intermediate Grades © 1997 Creative Teaching Press

Dear Parents,

Did You Know?

The daily newspaper is an excellent tool to help strengthen critical reading skills. By reading and discussing newsworthy topics, children improve their ability to summarize stories, identify important details, distinguish facts from opinions, and draw accurate conclusions. The following activity can strengthen your child's critical reading skills as he or she learns about real people and events.

How You Can Help

1. Cut out a short article that will interest your child. Fold the headline back so it can't be seen.

2. Ask your child to read the article. Invite him or her to write an "attention-grabbing" headline based on an important idea from the story.

3. Have your child compare the original headline with the one he or she wrote. Discuss how headlines must be clear, catchy, and convey the main idea of the article.

4. Practice with other articles. Reverse the process by showing your child headlines and having him or her predict story content.

5. Make a game out of matching headlines to articles. Cut off the headlines and place them in separate piles. Have your child read through headlines and stories to decide matches. Invite your child to share his or her problem-solving strategies.

6. To extend learning, invite your child to create his or her own neighborhood newspaper with friends. Have "reporters" write about exciting or unusual events happening at school or in your community. Encourage your child to use captivating, "eye-catching" headlines.

Parent Letters for the Intermediate Grades ©1997 Creative Teaching Press

Reading Comprehension

Dear Parents,

Did You Know?

When children read or hear different versions of the same story, they learn to appreciate and understand different points of view. They realize facts can appear different depending on who's presenting them. By examining different interpretations of a story, your child will also see the significance of supportive details when explaining the main idea. Use the following thought-provoking activities to help your child take a "second look" when comparing different versions of a story.

How You Can Help

1. Read aloud different versions of a myth, folktale, or fairy tale. Have your child compare similarities and differences in each interpretation. Ask questions such as:

   ● *What is the main idea of the story? Is the main idea the same in all versions?*
   ● *How does each author describe the main characters? In what way are the descriptions similar? different?*
   ● *Which version do you like best? Why?*

2. Have your child watch and compare videos of *Romeo and Juliet* and *West Side Story*. Ask your child to evaluate the similarities and differences in story setting, main idea, major characters portrayed, and lessons or morals.

3. Invite your child to assess different styles of reporting the news. Have him or her compare and contrast televised reports and newspaper versions of the same story.

4. Have family members write individual stories based on the same main story line. Decide on a main idea such as *Two children stow away on a rocket traveling to Mars. They meet martians who take them back to Earth.* After family members have written their stories, invite each person to share his or her version aloud. Compare the similarities and differences of the stories.

Parent Letters for the Intermediate Grades © 1997 Creative Teaching Press

Dear Parents,

Did You Know?

Children who know how to "skim" and "scan" reading material—glance through pages and look for specific words or phrases—find important facts more quickly. Skimming and scanning is especially handy when your child needs to locate specific facts for research projects. Use the following activity to help your child become a top-notch reader and researcher.

How You Can Help

1. Choose an article in a children's magazine. Read it in advance to determine the main idea of the story. For example, the main idea of an article titled *Calavaras County* may be the annual frog-jumping contest.

2. Ask your child to look through the magazine and locate the "mystery" article. Tell your child the main idea of the story, then show him or her how to quickly skim through articles looking for key words that would support the main idea. For example, *frog* and *contest*.

3. Set a time limit and invite your child to "beat the clock" by skimming through magazine articles to identify the mystery article before time runs out.

4. Choose new articles and repeat the process for additional practice. For extra challenge, reduce the amount of "search time" with each new round.

5. Adjust the activity to practice scanning. Instead of telling your child the main idea of one story, give him or her a list of notable words or phrases that can be found in various articles throughout the magazine. Invite your child to locate and circle the listed words before time runs out.

6. Help your child apply what was learned the next time he or she has a research report. Show your child how to skim through reference books to locate relevant articles and look for specific facts.

Reading Comprehension

Dear Parents,

Did You Know?

One of the most important steps of reading comes *after* your child puts the book down! You can help your child improve reading comprehension by encouraging him or her to think about and discuss what was read. When children reflect on what they've read, they clarify misunderstandings and remember important details that "fill in the gaps." The following suggestions will help your child "read between the lines" and get the most out of reading.

How You Can Help

1. Help your child become a more thoughtful reader by talking about stories in a natural, curious way. Make certain your child understands there are no right or wrong answers. Ask comparison questions such as:

    ● *How is the main character like you?*
    ● *How is the character's family the same as or different from ours?*
    ● *How is the main character's lifestyle similar to or different from yours?*
    ● *How is the setting of the story similar to or different from our neighborhood?*

2. Encourage your child to keep a reading journal. Have him or her jot down notes or draw illustrations about interesting or exciting details while reading. Invite your child to share journal entries with family members.

3. Invite your child to dramatize favorite stories. By acting out characters and events, your child will reevaluate and clarify key facts.

Parent Letters for the Intermediate Grades ©1997 Creative Teaching Press

Dear Parents,

Did You Know?

When children look at photographs, they can be strengthening important reading skills. Examining and comparing distinctive features of photographs is similar to identifying important details in a story. Both require use of descriptive words, the ability to separate key elements from less important details, the insight to distinguish fact from opinion, and the need to check for consistency. Use the following activity to help your child read with a "critical eye."

How You Can Help

1. Show your child an interesting photograph. Ask him or her to describe the picture, pointing out unusual or distinguishing features.

2. Play "Photo Detective" with your child by making statements about the picture and asking him or her to identify whether they're fact or opinion. For example, *There are two people in the picture* (fact); *The woman is the baby's mother* (opinion); *The baby is crying* (fact); *The baby is crying because he or she is sad* (opinion).

3. Switch roles and invite your child to give statements.

4. As a variation, use advertisements instead of photographs. For example, *The car is blue* (fact); *The interior room for passengers is outstanding* (opinion); *You have the option of either manual or automatic transmission* (fact).

5. Follow the same procedure the next time your child reads a story. Invite him or her to visualize what was read. Have your child use that mental picture to help him or her summarize important details from the story. Tell your child statements about the story and have him or her identify whether they're facts or opinions.

Reading Comprehension

Dear Parents,

Did You Know?

Reading becomes less of a struggle and more of a pleasure when you substitute "problem words" with simple, more familiar words. For example, the sentence *The man propelled the ball into the air* could be replaced with *The man threw the ball into the air.* By looking at story clues to decide replacement words, your child will read more smoothly, look for meaning behind words, and strengthen vocabulary skills. The following fun, simple activity will help your child read from start to finish with ease.

How You Can Help

1. Clip a short story from a children's magazine. Block out every fifth word throughout the story with black marker.

2. Invite your child to read the story, replacing blocked words with new ones—the goal is to read a story that makes sense, not identify the "hidden" words.

3. After reading the story aloud, discuss word choices. Have your child identify which "story clues" were helpful when deciding word replacements.

4. As an alternative approach, give your child possible replacement words. Ask him or her to read the story to decide which words make sense and which do not.

5. For extra fun, invite your child to write silly "word-out" stories to share with friends and family members. Have him or her block out nouns, verbs, adjectives, or adverbs, then ask for replacement words without reading the story aloud —only the parts of speech for block-out words are given as clues (e.g., *I need a noun to complete the next sentence*). Invite your child to read the humorous results aloud.

Parent Letters for the Intermediate Grades ©1997 Creative Teaching Press

Dear Parents,

Did You Know?

Story puzzles not only intrigue children, but also strengthen important reading and problem-solving skills. When children solve puzzles, they read every step of the way—looking for word clues, checking to make sure sentences are placed in logical order, and reading the finished product for overall clarity and meaning. Use the following fun, hands-on activity the next time your child "puzzles" over reading.

How You Can Help

1. Cut out a few magazine stories several paragraphs long. Glue each to different-colored construction paper.

2. Cut each story into random slices—four to six lines per slice. Store each set in separate envelopes.

3. Give your child an envelope and ask him or her to reassemble the story. Help your child look for "word clues" to decide the correct order. For example, if one story slice ends with the incomplete sentence *lions, tigers, and . . .*, the next strip should begin with an animal name to complete the thought.

4. Repeat the process with other story envelopes. After putting together the stories, have your child read them aloud.

5. As a challenging variation, have your child reassemble more than one story at a time.

6. To extend learning, invite your child to create new story slicers for friends and family members to enjoy.

Parent Letters for the Intermediate Grades ©1997 Creative Teaching Press

Reading Comprehension

Dear Parents,

Did You Know?

Children who read from "different perspectives" look at written words more carefully and thoughtfully. When your child examines stories from the author's perspective, he or she learns to distinguish facts from opinions, reexamine story content for specific details, and apply this knowledge to his or her own writing. The following activity will help expand your child's imagination and encourage him or her to "read between the lines."

How You Can Help

1. After reading a book, have your child pretend to be the author. Invite him or her to dress the role and act the part.

2. Conduct an author interview. Stir your child's imagination and critical-thinking skills by asking questions such as:

    ● *Why did you write this book?*
    ● *How did you want the audience to feel after reading your book?*
    ● *What lessons do you hope people learn from your book?*
    ● *What would you like your fans to know about you?*

3. Videotape or audiotape the interview, and invite your child to review the performance.

4. Have your child write to the author of the book.

5. Encourage your child to think of specific goals before writing his or her own story. Ask questions such as *Is there a special reason for writing the story? How do you want the audience to feel after reading the story? What are some ways to accomplish this goal?*

Parent Letters for the Intermediate Grades ©1997 Creative Teaching Press

Dear Parents,

Did You Know?

Children become better readers when exposed to different kinds of reading through everyday activities. Your child will better understand the "flexibility" of written language when he or she sees it used for different purposes such as giving directions, selling a product, or sharing an opinion. The following fun, simple ideas will help your child practice reading skills and appreciate the many "faces" of written language.

How You Can Help

1. Have your child skim recipes as you prepare favorite treats. Ask him or her to tell you how much of each item to add, the oven setting, and how long to cook the food.

2. Have your child help select items from mail-order catalogs. Ask him or her to read through descriptions to find the price, choice of colors, or any other distinguishing characteristics.

3. Invite your child to put reading skills to use the next time you throw a party. Have him or her read the guest list aloud as you check off RSVPs, skim through "party planners" for fun games, and read birthday cards aloud for others to hear and enjoy.

4. Recruit your child's help the next time you pay your bills. Not only will your child get practical reading experience, he or she will receive an eye-opening lesson on the value of a dollar.

Reading Application

Dear Parents,

Did You Know?

Road trips can provide wonderful reading opportunities. While on the road, your child is motivated to read such items as travel guides, road maps, street signs, bumper stickers, and restaurant menus. These real-life experiences not only show the importance of reading, but also strengthen fact-finding and research skills that carry over into other subject areas. Encourage your child to play "tour guide" the next time your family plans an outing.

How You Can Help

1. Give your child a list of travel destinations, and invite him or her to choose the place for your next family trip. Encourage your child to read about each possibility before choosing the location.

2. Have your child locate the area on a map. Decide together which route is the best. As you travel to your destination, have your child read aloud names of roads and highways to help keep you "on track."

3. Encourage your child and other family members to read billboards, bumper stickers, license plates, and store windows as you travel. Invite them to spot

   - silly slogans.
   - funny bumper stickers.
   - names of different states.
   - strange store names.
   - any words in ABC order. (For example, the word *apple* on a grocery store window, followed by the word *bend* on a road sign, then the word *car* written on a billboard, and so on.)

4. Have your child read tour pamphlets and guides to discover historical landmarks, exquisite restaurants, and unusual tourist attractions for your family to visit.

5. Encourage your child to record memorable events in a travel journal. Invite him or her to read aloud and share entries with friends and family members upon returning home.

Parent Letters for the Intermediate Grades ©1997 Creative Teaching Press

Dear Parents,

Did You Know?

Books are an excellent way to teach your child important life lessons. Children are more eager to learn the "do's and don'ts" when presented in the context of a story. Older children in particular are more motivated to read when story characters struggle with real-life issues and problems. The following activity shows your child that even fun, entertaining stories can offer important lessons to live by.

How You Can Help

1. Collect fables and folktales from around the world. Choose ones that teach valuable lessons, such as *The Boy Who Cried Wolf* by Aesop, *The Gold Coin* by Ada Alma, and *Our King Has Horns!* by Richard Peaver.

2. Read a fable or folktale aloud to your child. Stop before you reach the ending, and ask your child to identify the problem or dilemma facing the main character.

3. Invite your child to predict two possible endings to the story—one involving the "right" way to solve the problem, and the other involving the "wrong" way.

4. Finish reading the tale and discuss the lesson together. Have your child give an example of how that lesson may help him or her in real life. For example, *The Boy Who Cried Wolf* teaches the reader that if you always lie, people may not believe you when you finally tell the truth.

5. Share and enjoy other fables and folktales with your child. Encourage him or her to look for "lessons to learn" in every piece of literature. Invite your child to share the new-found knowledge with other family members.

Reading Application

Dear Parents,

Did You Know?

Keeping a diary not only encourages your child to write, but also to read. When children keep a diary, they write about the most exciting subject of all—themselves! Diaries motivate children to read through their writing, reflect on thoughts and ideas, and evaluate situations more critically. Use the following suggestions to help your child get started.

How You Can Help

1. Get your child comfortable with the idea of keeping a diary by starting off with a "study journal."

2. Encourage your child to write notes in the journal as he or she reads and studies for school. Invite your child to jot down interesting quotes, questions that come to mind, or any other observations.

3. Give your child the option of keeping the study journal private, or giving it to you to write positive feedback. Encourage your child to use these notes as study guides when preparing for tests or completing research reports.

4. As your child feels more comfortable recording thoughts and ideas in writing, encourage him or her to keep a personal diary. Explain how writing down thoughts, ideas, and emotions helps a person think through and evaluate problems more thoroughly.

5. Respect your child's wish to keep diary entries private. When your child volunteers to share something from the diary, respond positively and invite him or her to tell you more about what was written.

Parent Letters for the Intermediate Grades ©1997 Creative Teaching Press

Dear Parents,

Did You Know?

Children are much more intrigued and excited about reading when they identify with story characters. By comparing characters to real individuals, with feelings and actions similar to their own, children are motivated to read and learn more about them. The following fun, thought-provoking activity will help bring storybook characters "to life."

How You Can Help

1. Read together a book from a series, such as *Ramona the Pest, Fudge,* or *Little House on the Prairie.*

2. Have your child describe each character's personality. Ask him or her questions such as *What do you like about him or her? What don't you like? Would you be friends with him or her? Why or why not? In what ways are you similar? different?*

3. Write real-life situations on index cards. For example:

   - You found a wallet on the street.
   - You and a friend accidentally broke your mother's favorite dish.
   - You forgot to study for a test.
   - You really want to go to a party, but you already promised to baby-sit your little brother.
   - A bully is teasing you at school.
   - Your little sister follows you wherever you go.

4. Invite your child to pick situation cards and explain or act out how each story character would handle the situation. Have your child compare these behaviors to those he or she would show under the same circumstances.

5. Encourage your child to read more books from the same series and share what he or she learned.

Parent Letters for the Intermediate Grades ©1997 Creative Teaching Press

Reading Application

Dear Parents,

Did You Know?

You can help your child become a better reader by providing practical opportunities to use reading and writing skills. Children understand and appreciate the importance of reading when they observe and use it in daily routines. The following quick, simple activities will help your child see and experience the advantages of reading in the real world.

How You Can Help

1. Have your child browse through collections of coupons, newspaper advertisements, and catalogs. Invite him or her to find discounts on items your family uses. You may choose to give your child the savings as an incentive.

2. Invite your child to be the family "mail carrier." Have him or her collect and sort through mail, distributing letters and advertisements to family members.

3. Encourage your child to read food labels and learn about important nutritional facts.

4. Instead of buying ready-made materials, have your child read directions to put pieces together. Encourage him or her to skim through directions, then carefully reread each section step-by-step.

5. Keep alert for news stories that may interest your child. Encourage him or her to follow the news through different medias—TV, radio, and newspapers. Invite your child to write "special reports" to read aloud to family members.

Parent Letters for the Intermediate Grades © 1997 Creative Teaching Press

Dear Parents,

Did You Know?

When you read stories aloud to your child, you help him or her learn proper grammar and sentence structure. Your child can hear when words and phrases don't "sound right." By listening to stories and developing an "ear" for language, your child will be more successful at self-assessing his or her own writing.

How You Can Help

1. In advance, tape-record a favorite short story. As you make the recording, include several errors. For example, mispronounce some words, use incorrect verbs, omit ending marks or commas, and change sentence sequence.

2. Tell your child in advance how many errors there are in the recording. Invite him or her to find all the errors. Have your child identify each mistake as it is heard, or take notes and discuss findings at the end of the recording.

3. If your child has difficulty hearing the errors, read the passage correctly for comparison.

4. For more of a challenge, don't tell your child the number of errors in the recording—invite him or her to give you the final count.

5. Repeat the process using your child's writing. Invite him or her to read the writing sample aloud into the tape recorder, then play it back and listen for errors. As errors are identified, help your child make corrections to his or her writing.

Dear Parents,

Did You Know?

Sharing thoughts and opinions with others improves speaking, listening, and writing skills. When children "talk about it," they clarify their thinking, learn from listening to others, and generate creative ideas to use in their writing. The next time friends visit, try the following high-energy "talk" game as a conversation starter.

How You Can Help

1. Divide players into two teams, and give each person paper and a pencil.

2. Choose one person to be the "talker" and another person to "referee."

3. For two minutes, ask the "talker" to mentally brainstorm facts about a particular person, place, or thing while other players secretly write their ideas on paper. Encourage players to write one- or two-word details. For example, if the topic is baseball, a person could write *bat, players, bases, innings, score*, and *home run*.

4. At the signal, have the talker share all he or she knows about the topic in one minute. Ask players to circle words on their list that match what the talker says.

5. Have the referee take notes about facts shared aloud. Use these "records" to verify what players circled.

6. Have each team share what they circled. The team with the most matches wins one point.

7. Play again using a new topic, talker, and referee. The first team to earn five points wins the game.

8. As a variation, choose people, places, and things found in favorite books. For example, Willy Wonka, Prince Charming's castle, or Aladdin's lamp.

> Bat, baseball, home run, bases...

Parent Letters for the Intermediate Grades ©1997 Creative Teaching Press

Dear Parents,

Did You Know?

Writing is easier when you talk about ideas before writing them down. Children feel more relaxed and motivated about writing when they have opportunities to share and discuss ideas before jotting them down on paper. Help your child be a better writer by asking thought-provoking questions and responding to his or her ideas enthusiastically. Use the following mind-teaser activity to make "creative talk" a family affair.

How You Can Help

1. Ask family members imaginative "What if?" questions about favorite fairy tales and fables. For example:

   - *What if King Midas had a peanut-butter touch?*
   - *What if Rumpelstilskin forgot how to spin straw into gold?*
   - *What if Rapunzel had short, curly hair that never grew long?*

2. Switch roles and have family members take turns asking "What if?" questions for others to answers.

3. Invite your child to use discussion ideas to write his or her own "fractured fairy tales and fables." Encourage him or her to be descriptive and humorous in the revisions.

4. Invite your child to read aloud the revised stories for family members to enjoy.

5. Extend the activity to ask "What if?" questions about current happenings, historical events, or future possibilities. For example:

   - *What if society ran out of gasoline?*
   - *What if electricity was never discovered?*
   - *What if computers could carry on conversations?*

Speaking and Listening

Dear Parents,

Did You Know?

A key ingredient in both oral language and creative writing is "descriptive details." These describing words help us visualize people, places, and things described in stories (for example, *slimy* snail, *rickety* house, and *glass* slipper). The following family activity helps your child discover new descriptive words to "spice up" both speaking and writing skills.

How You Can Help

1. Have family members write names of people, places, and things on separate index cards. Collect and shuffle the cards, then place them in a pile, face down.

2. Invite your child to select a card from the top of the pile. Have him or her give descriptive clues as others try to guess the word written on the card. For example, descriptive clues for *Pinocchio* may include *wooden boy, long nose,* and *puppet.*

3. Have family members take turns selecting words and giving clues.

4. As an alternative, divide the family into teams and play a timed game of Clue. Give each group half the cards and see which team can guess the most amount of words in fifteen seconds.

Parent Letters for the Intermediate Grades © 1997 Creative Teaching Press

Dear Parents,

Did You Know?

Help your child strengthen both listening and writing skills by telling funny, entertaining stories. Storytelling and creative writing have similar "guidelines"—an attention-getting introduction, a plot that is easy to follow, vivid details to captivate the audience, and a dramatic ending. One of the best places to get storytelling ideas is the family photo album. Take your child on a trip down "memory lane" as you help him or her improve both oral language and writing skills.

How You Can Help

1. Gather an assortment of old family photos.

2. Invite your child to select one of the photos. Have him or her make guesses about the time, place, and circumstances in which the photograph was taken.

3. Tell your child about the photograph. Share your favorite story about the person or place captured on film. Include "juicy" details and fun facts to capture your child's interest and illustrate the use of descriptive words.

4. Invite your child to help rearrange photos in chronological order. Have him or her write descriptive sentences underneath each picture in the photo album.

5. To extend learning, invite your child to help you make a Family History Book by recording facts in a journal.

Parent Letters for the Intermediate Grades ©1997 Creative Teaching Press

Dear Parents,

Did You Know?

You may have heard the familiar expression, *A picture is worth a thousand words.* But did you know your child can improve his or her writing skills just by looking at and talking about pictures? When children compare and describe similarities and differences in photographs, they learn the importance of descriptive details in creative writing. You'll be amazed at the creative and imaginative stories your child will create just by looking at pictures of unknown people and places.

How You Can Help

1. Have your child cut out magazine pictures of people and places.

2. Choose one picture and model the excitement of storytelling. Weave an imaginative story around the person or place shown. Invite your child to add his or her own descriptive words or creative details.

3. Have your child select a picture to use in his or her own make-believe story. Encourage your child's creativity and imagination by asking questions such as *Who is in the picture? Why is he or she there? Who is taking the picture? What happened just before the picture was taken? What happened next?*

4. After your child shares the story aloud, encourage him or her to write it down on paper. Invite your child to use the picture to illustrate the story.

5. As an alternative activity, have your child use his or her imagination to describe newspaper photos. Invite your child to guess the circumstances in which pictures were taken, and describe the emotions portrayed in each photo. Read together the articles that correspond with the photographs to see how closely your child's descriptions match actual events.

Parent Letters for the Intermediate Grades © 1997 Creative Teaching Press

Dear Parents,

Did You Know?

The best way to encourage and motivate your child to write is to have him or her write about familiar topics. Children often experience "writer's block" when they struggle with ideas to write about. The next time your child says, *I can't think of anything to write about*, encourage him or her to write about familiar topics such as a fun family trip, an embarrassing moment, a favorite hobby, or a lovable pet. Use the following activity to invite your whole family to join in the fun!

How You Can Help

1. Place a notebook and pencil where it's accessible to every family member.

2. After dinner (or another convenient time), jot down the date and a few comments about the day's events.

3. Encourage your child and other family members to write in the "diary" daily—but don't force it. The less pressure, the more enthusiastic your child will be about contributing.

4. Give your child encouraging feedback by writing comments alongside his or her diary entries, or invite him or her to share entries aloud.

Dear Parents,

Did You Know?

Creative writing begins by freeing the imagination. It's something everyone has, but grows weak and ineffective when used infrequently. Every time your child "flexes" imagination muscles, he or she expands his or her creative writing skills. Here's a creative writing activity sure to catch your child's attention—writing a letter to his or her future self!

How You Can Help

1. Have your child and other family members write letters dated ten or twenty years into the future. Ask each person to use his or her imagination to write about future topics such as

   - a description of his or her home and neighborhood.
   - the excitement of working in his or her career.
   - advice on how to raise children.
   - descriptions of friends, coworkers, and neighbors.

2. Invite your child and other family members to share their letters aloud.

3. Seal the letters and put them away in a safe place. Ten or twenty years from now, share the letters at a letter-opening reunion!

Parent Letters for the Intermediate Grades ©1997 Creative Teaching Press

Dear Parents,

Did You Know?

When children are told to "be more descriptive," they don't always understand what it means. Children need to see and hear examples before they can understand what "descriptive" means. One way to help your child hear the difference between descriptive and nondescriptive writing is to read aloud sentences in which verbs and adjectives have been omitted. For example, the sentence *The wild rapids came crashing down on the small, shabby raft* would read *The rapids came down on the raft.* Another approach is to connect art to writing—to "draw" story sentences to "see" the importance of descriptive details.

How You Can Help

1. Say aloud a simple sentence such as *See the dog.* Have both you and your child draw separate pictures to go with the sentence.

2. Compare and discuss why your pictures look different. Explain how using descriptive words such as *small, black,* and *spotted* would have made the sentence clearer.

3. Write another simple sentence on paper. For example, *The man and the woman went for a walk in the park.* Have your child read the sentence aloud. Ask him or her the following questions.

   ● *Can you picture the scene clearly in your mind?*

   ● *Do you think my mental picture of the scene is the same as yours? Why or why not?*

   ● *Could you draw a detailed picture on paper using only the facts given in the sentence? Why or why not? What can be done to the sentence to make it clearer?*

4. Invite your child to add "descriptive clues" as you draw a picture to match the sentence. For example, *The tall, skinny man and the short, plump woman went for a brisk walk in the tree-covered park.*

5. Repeat the activity with a new sentence, switching roles and inviting your child to draw the picture as you give clues.

6. As an extension, have your child tell a descriptive story as you act out the sentences. Switch roles and invite your child to "take center stage."

Dear Parents,

Did You Know?

Every time you sit down to write, you teach your child an important lesson. Whether you're writing a phone message, paying a bill, or jotting down a shopping list, you're showing your child that writing serves a purpose. Help your child improve writing skills by getting him or her involved with real-life writing experiences. A natural "kid motivator" is letter writing. Children are eager to write letters because they love to receive mail!

How You Can Help

1. Invite your child to look through and select ten favorite greeting cards from a stationery store.

2. Have him or her write messages in the cards and send them to friends and relatives.

3. To encourage others to write back, invite your child to include jokes, riddles, puzzles, and "secret codes" in the letters. Have your child skim through riddle books to find fun "ticklers" to share with others.

4. Invite your child to read the letters sent by others. Encourage him or her to continue corresponding on a regular basis.

5. To add a cultural twist to the letter-writing experience, invite your child to write to pen pals living in different countries. Have your child visit your local library and look through children's magazines (e.g., *1, 2, 3, Contact; Jack and Jill Magazine; Read for the Fun of It*) to find international addresses.

Parent Letters for the Intermediate Grades ©1997 Creative Teaching Press

Dear Parents,

Did You Know?

One of the most difficult parts of writing is just getting started—children often get "stuck" before they begin. The next time your child gets "writer's block," turn on some classical music! Listening to and interpreting music not only soothes and calms inspiring writers, it arouses artistry and imagination!

How You Can Help

1. Have your child listen to music. Choose instrumental music so he or she can concentrate on the melody without the distraction of words.

2. Invite your child to close his or her eyes while listening to the first few minutes of the song.

3. As the song continues, have your child open his or her eyes and draw whatever comes to mind. If your child hesitates, encourage him or her to start with colors and shapes, then move on to more detailed drawings.

4. After the song is finished, invite your child to share and discuss the drawing. Ask your child to describe the thoughts he or she had while listening to the music.

5. Invite your child to write his or her thoughts on paper. Encourage him or her to write poetry or create a story revolving around musical impressions.

6. Repeat the activity with other kinds of music. Invite your child to compare how various melodies evoke different thoughts and feelings.

Dear Parents,

Did You Know?

Brainstorming is a strategy used by businessmen, scientists, writers, and other problem solvers to help generate ideas. It involves listing all ideas on a topic that come to mind without judging whether they are good or bad. The next time your child says, *I don't know what to write about*, try this brainstorming activity to help him or her get started.

How You Can Help

1. Ask family members to collect small "secret" objects and bring them to a table.

2. Have one person hold up his or her object for others to see. Ask family members to write as many uses for that object they can think of in five minutes. For example, a tin can could be used as a pencil holder, cookie cutter, dough roller, vase, drum, a doll's body, or a measuring cup.

3. Take turns sharing and comparing brainstorming ideas. See who comes up with the longest list.

4. Extend the activity by having family members write "how-to" directions for their ideas.

5. For added fun, invite family members to "swap" directions. Take turns reading directions aloud, then use them to make some of the creative crafts.

Parent Letters for the Intermediate Grades ©1997 Creative Teaching Press

Dear Parents,

Did You Know?

When children play word games, they not only have fun, but also improve their vocabulary skills! Children learn, retain, and recall new words more easily when taught in a fun, relaxing environment. Invite family and friends to play the following version of Password, and watch your child's enthusiasm for new words grow.

How You Can Help

1. Divide players into two teams.

2. Assign yourself as "quiz master," and choose a secret word for teams to guess.

3. Whisper the word to team leaders.

4. Invite players to guess the secret word by listening to one-word clues given by team leaders. Clues may include similar words (disease, illness), opposites (up, down), descriptive words (hairy for ape), and "key" words (pacifier for baby).

5. The first team to guess the word earns one point.

6. Invite someone else to be quiz master and change leaders. Continue playing until one team gets ten points.

7. As an alternative, play one-on-one with your child—take turns picking words and giving the other person clues. Try setting a new time record with each new word.

8. For an extra challenge, ask players to spell secret words correctly to earn bonus points.

Vocabulary and Spelling

Dear Parents,

Did You Know?

Developing a strong vocabulary is important in all levels of communication. Whether writing a report, giving directions, or speaking to an audience, children who possess large "word banks" are more successful at expressing their ideas and concerns to others. Use the following outdoor activities to help your child experience the wonderful world of words.

How You Can Help

1. Visit new and interesting places with your child. Talk about what you see and encourage your child to ask questions.

2. Use an occasional specialized or technical word in your answers and discussion. Your child is more likely to remember these words when they tie into fun, real-life experiences.

3. As you explore and discover new and unusual places, invite your child to find words in ABC order. For example, while visiting a museum, your child may see words such as *aborigine, buffalo,* and *chapel* in display cases.

4. Invent imaginative names for businesses you see during your outings. For example, *Pick and Lick Ice Cream Parlor, Wheeler Dealer Bike Shop,* and *Nuts to You Hardware.*

5. Invite your child to spot "stumper" words to challenge your knowledge.

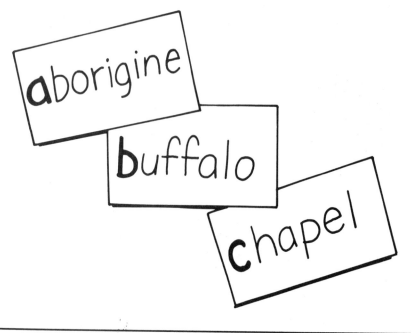

Parent Letters for the Intermediate Grades © 1997 Creative Teaching Press

Dear Parents,

Did You Know?

Secret codes are a great way to have fun while reinforcing important language-arts skills. Children are so caught up in the excitement of solving mystery messages, they are unaware of practicing valuable decoding skills as well as adding new words to their vocabulary. The following fun, interactive activities will help your child become a top-notch reading "decoder."

How You Can Help

1. Write out secret messages by substituting numbers for letters—*1* for *A*, *2* for *B*, *3* for *C*, and so on. Invite your child to "break the code."

2. Write words or messages in "phone code" using numbers on the dial to replace letters. For example, the word *ball* would be *2255* in phone code.

3. Be aware that each number stands for more than one letter (e.g., number *2* represents letters *A*, *B*, and *C*). Explain to your child that each code may have more than one solution. For example, code *2255* could translate to *ball* or *call*. Your child will need to look at the context of the message to determine which words to choose.

4. Encourage your child to invent original codes for friends and family members to translate and read.

5. Invite your child to learn more about codes by reading books such as *Codes for Kids* by Burton Albert, *All Kinds of Codes* by Walt Babson, *Codes and Ciphers: Secret Writing through the Ages* by John Laffin, and *How to Write Codes and Send Messages* by John Peterson.

Vocabulary and Spelling

Dear Parents,

Did You Know?

Maintaining a playful attitude about words can help your child build a strong vocabulary. When children think of learning new words as a game rather than a chore, they are much more willing and eager to expand their knowledge. Motivate your child to learn new words and improve spelling skills by playing games such as the following.

How You Can Help

1. Give each player a copy of the attached grid. Cut out all sets of alphabet letters and place them face down on the table.

2. Take turns choosing 25 letters. Have players use the letters to write words horizontally, vertically, or diagonally on the grids—all players use the same letters, but may form different words.

3. Ask players to exchange papers and find "hidden" words in the puzzle. Award one point for each letter of a word (for example, *lunch* would be worth five points).

4. Encourage your child to use a dictionary to check for word spellings.

5. The player with the most points wins.

6. Play again using new grids. For variation, set a time limit for finding words.

Parent Letters for the Intermediate Grades © 1997 Creative Teaching Press

Five-by-Five

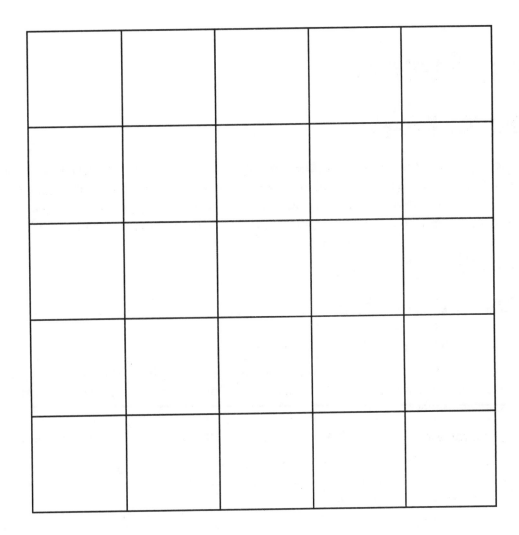

A	B	C	D	E	F	G	H	I
J	K	L	M	N	O	P	Q	R
S	T	U	V	W	X	Y	Z	

Vocabulary and Spelling

Dear Parents,

Did You Know?

If spelling practice is a dreaded chore in your household, surprise your child by pulling out a board game! Games such as Scrabble, Boggle, Wheel of Fortune, and Hangman are excellent for improving spelling skills. Children are more motivated to look at words carefully, compare spelling patterns, and remember letter sequence when playing a game or solving a puzzle. Use the following family game to sharpen your child's spelling skills.

How You Can Help

1. Have each family member draw a nine-box grid as shown.

2. Ask players to fill their grids with words, one letter per box. They may start words in any box and add letters in any direction as long as letters are placed in correct spelling sequence.

3. Once grids are complete, have players switch puzzles and try to identify the other person's words.

4. Repeat the activity using 12- or 15-box grids. Encourage family members to use a dictionary to find unusual words.

5. As a variation, pick a word "theme," for example, animal names, sporting events, or book characters.

6. For more challenge, have each player use words that share beginning and ending letters. For example, if a player writes the word *bear* in his or her grid, the word *rabbit* could follow since it begins with the letter *r*.

ELEPHANTS

Parent Letters for the Intermediate Grades © 1997 Creative Teaching Press

Dear Parents,

Did You Know?

Solving word puzzles strengthens and expands both critical-thinking and vocabulary skills. Children are more motivated to learn and use new words when having fun. Any kind of word puzzle or game encourages your child to read new words, seek out word definitions, look at spelling patterns, and connect new words to those already learned. The following word challenge shows how puzzles can increase your child's vocabulary.

How You Can Help

1. Distribute paper and pencils. Have both you and your child write the alphabet at the top of the paper.

2. Secretly think of a five-letter word and ask your child to do the same.

3. Ask your child to guess your word. Tell your child how many letters in his or her guess are in your secret word. For example, if your word is *chair* and your child guesses *couch*, two letters are correct. Encourage your child to write down and keep track of guesses, recording how many letters are correct (e.g., *couch*—2).

4. Take turns guessing each other's words. Encourage your child to use his or her "notes" and the process of elimination to make educated guesses.

5. Encourage your child to cross off alphabet letters at the top of his or her page to keep track of eliminated letters. For example, if your child guesses the word *couch* and your word is *pizza*, he or she crosses off letters *c, o, u,* and *h* from the alphabet list because none of the letters are correct.

6. Whichever player guesses the other person's secret word first wins.

7. As your child becomes more skilled at this game, try using six-, seven-, or eight-letter words.

Vocabulary and Spelling

Dear Parents,

Did You Know?

Dictionaries are excellent resources for learning new words, but rarely do children get excited when they hear the words, *Look it up!* That's because most children view using dictionaries as a bothersome chore rather than a gateway to new knowledge and fun. Help your child get more pleasure from dictionaries by making a game out of looking up and using new words.

How You Can Help

1. Every morning, randomly select a word from the dictionary. Flip through the pages until your child says, *Stop.* Invite him or her to tell you which column and how far down to look on the selected page. For example, *Second column, twelfth word down.*

2. Read the definition together, including the pronunciation and the part of speech. Discuss different ways the word can be used in a sentence and look at the sample sentences given.

3. Challenge your child and other family members to use the word at least three times throughout the day. (You may wish to have your child write the "daily word" on a piece of paper and keep it in his or her pocket as a reminder.)

4. Invite your child to keep a "word journal" to record ways he or she uses the word throughout the day. This not only serves as a "memory refresher" when you discuss the day's events, but also becomes a valuable resource for future writing and reading assignments.

5. At the end of the day, share and compare ways family members used the daily word.

6. To extend the activity, create your own family dictionary of daily words.

Parent Letters for the Intermediate Grades ©1997 Creative Teaching Press

Vocabulary and Spelling

Dear Parents,

Did You Know?

Creative thinkers enjoy "playing" with new ideas. They challenge themselves to look for new approaches and "hidden" meanings. This is also true of creative writers—they enjoy using words in new and unusual ways through brain teasers and word puzzles. Use the following "eye-catching" activities to help your child strengthen word-recognition skills.

How You Can Help

1. Construct words or phrases to give visual clues to their meanings. For example, banana written as a broken word *ban ana* represents "banana split." Use the following puzzles to help you get started.

   <u>book</u>
   due   (answer: book overdue)

   <u>man</u>
   board   (answer: man overboard)

   sideside   (answer: side by side)

   egsg   (answer: scrambled eggs)

   _____ et   (blanket)

   O hole NE   (answer: hole in one)

2. Invite your child to discover and write palindromes—words that are spelled the same backward and forward. For example, *radar, otto, madam,* and *Adam.*

3. Invite your child to create Hink Pinks—riddles with rhyming word pairs for answers. Try these to get started.

   - What do you call a chubby kitty? (fat cat)
   - What do you call a crying father? (sad dad)
   - What do you call a desk that doesn't fall down? (stable table)
   - What do you call a rabbit who tells jokes? (funny bunny)

Dear Parents,

Did You Know?

Children who look for patterns in words are more successful spellers. Help your child learn and remember correct spelling by pointing out and grouping similar words together. (For example, *train, chain,* and *pain.*) Your child will also improve spelling and vocabulary skills by completing fun, word-building activities like the following.

How You Can Help

1. Secretly think of a word, then write down the first letter. For example, *r* for the word *rose.*

2. Ask your child to privately think of another word that begins with your letter *(r),* then add the next letter of his or her word. For example, *ro* for the word *robot.*

3. Continue the process of adding new letters. Explain to your child that every time another letter is added, he or she may need to think of a new word to fit the pattern. For example, if you add the letter *s* to form *ros,* the word *robot* will no longer work.

4. Although both you and your child should think of new words as letters are added, the goal of the game is to get the *other player* to complete a word first—if a player "accidentally" completes a word, he or she loses the round.

5. Another way a round ends is by declaring a "word challenge." This is done when one player thinks the other is "bluffing"—adding letters without any word in mind. If the opponent is unable to say a word that fits the letter pattern, he or she loses the round. If he or she correctly identifies a word, he or she wins the round.

6. Each time a player loses a round, he or she must write the next letter in the word *ghost*—the letter *g* with the first loss, letter *h* with the second, and so on. The player who gets his or her opponent to spell the word *ghost* first is declared the champion.

Parent Letters for the Intermediate Grades ©1997 Creative Teaching Press

Dear Parents,

Did You Know?

Children learn thousands of words simply by listening to and discussing ideas with others. By talking to your child often, inserting new vocabulary words in the conversations, and inviting your child to ask questions, your child's vocabulary will increase naturally and effortlessly. The next time your family is sitting around the dinner table, try these brain stretchers to stir up conversation.

How You Can Help

1. Invite family members to look at simple objects and events in new and unusual ways. For example:

   ● Describe ice cream to someone who has never seen or tasted it.
   ● Brainstorm ways to improve a paper clip.
   ● List 25 uses for a spoon.
   ● Write and read aloud a poem that explains how darkness sounds.

2. Prepare your own family debate. Have two family members debate the pros and cons of an issue. Invite other members to listen and offer feedback.

3. Invite family members to listen for and identify your "secret" word. Mentally choose a word, then use it in the course of conversation. Family members will catch on when they hear you repeat the word several times throughout the night!

4. Invite your child and other family members to think of additional brain stretchers—the more outlandish the better!

tasty

sticky

wet

sweet

cold

smooth

Vocabulary and Spelling

Dear Parents,

Did You Know?

Manipulatives strengthen math skills. They are the proof children need to verify memorized facts. For example, two groups of three apples proves that 2 x 3 = 6. When children can "translate" written problems using pictures or objects, they "think" math rather than memorize numbers. Use the following hands-on activity to help your child get beyond memorization into understanding multiplication facts.

How You Can Help

1. Give your child a handful of toothpicks.

2. Dictate several multiplication problems such as 4 x 3.

3. Have your child lay four toothpicks side by side in a vertical row. Ask him or her to place three more toothpicks in a horizontal row on top of the others to form a criss-cross grid.

4. Invite your child to count the intersection points on the toothpick grid to find the answer to the problem (12).

5. Ask your child to reverse the order of the toothpicks to show 3 x 4—three toothpicks on the bottom, four on top. Have him or her count the intersection points to prove that 4 x 3 is the same as 3 x 4.

6. Repeat the process with additional multiplication problems. Use larger numbers to increase the difficulty—you may choose to have your child draw criss-cross lines rather than use toothpicks for larger multiplication problems.

7. Encourage your child to use this pictorial version of multiplication to double-check numerical calculations.

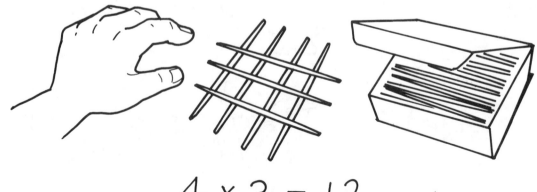

$$4 \times 3 = 12$$

Parent Letters for the Intermediate Grades   ©1997 Creative Teaching Press

Dear Parents,

Did You Know?

Number facts—addition, subtraction, multiplication, and division—are needed at every level of mathematics. Whether it's figuring out a geometry problem or calculating cooking time for a turkey, children who know number facts "by heart" solve problems more quickly and successfully. The following dice game is just one of many interactive games you can use to help your child practice number facts easily and effortlessly.

How You Can Help

1. Write numbers 1–40 on the attached grid.

2. Have your child roll three dice. Ask him or her to add, subtract, multiply, and/or divide the numbers shown to equal any grid number. For example, if your child rolls a three, five, and six, he or she may cover the number *ten*, since 5 x 6 = 30 and 30 ÷ 3 = 10. Cover grid numbers with paper pieces.

3. Take turns rolling the dice and "winning" grid numbers, earning one point for each number covered.

4. Award bonus points when a winning number is directly adjacent to one already covered.

5. Continue until all numbers are covered. The player with the most points wins.

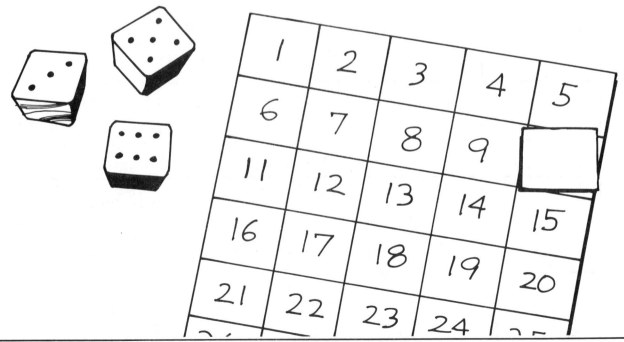

Three-Dice Throw

Parent Letters for the Intermediate Grades © 1997 Creative Teaching Press

Dear Parents,

Did You Know?

Calculators are valuable math tools, but they do not eliminate the need for children to know number facts. Punching numbers into a calculator doesn't always work—the wrong number or function key may be used accidentally. By knowing number facts, your child will be able to think through math problems and decide if answers make sense. Use the following pattern activity to help your child practice number facts and think through calculations carefully.

How You Can Help

1. Write single-digit numbers 1–9 in random order across the top row of the attached grid.

2. Make a "secret rule" for changing each top-row number, and write new numbers in the second row. For example, multiply all numbers by three.

3. Use a new rule to fill in the third row, this time leaving a few boxes blank. Repeat the process for other rows.

4. Use the first two rows to show your child how to compare numbers to determine the secret rule. Invite him or her to identify secret rules for other rows, then follow the patterns to fill in blank boxes.

5. Have your child check calculations with a calculator. Ask him or her to recalculate answers that do not match.

6. Make the game more difficult by using a secret rule that involves more than one operation. For example, multiply by two, then add five.

7. Invite your child to use a new grid to make number patterns for other family members to "decode."

Parent Letters for the Intermediate Grades ©1997 Creative Teaching Press

Number Facts

What's My Rule?

Parent Letters for the Intermediate Grades ©1997 Creative Teaching Press

Dear Parents,

Did You Know?

Estimating is making an "educated guess." When children estimate, they determine an approximate answer based on prior knowledge. For example, if your child knows it takes fifteen minutes to solve ten problems, he or she can estimate the time to complete twenty (twice the time, or 1/2 hour). Help your child strengthen estimation skills by practicing them in real-life situations. Try this tasty activity to help you get started.

How You Can Help

1. Show your child several different-sized containers such as a film canister, coffee can, jar, glass, small bowl, and large bowl.

2. Invite your child to guess and record how many popcorn pieces fill a film canister (or other small container).

3. Make a large bowl of popcorn. Ask your child to count the number of popcorn pieces needed to fill the canister. Have him or her compare the number to his or her estimate.

4. Invite your child to estimate how much popcorn is needed to fill other containers (coffee can, jar, small bowl). Show him or her a shortcut by estimating the number of popcorn-filled containers it takes to fill each new container. For example, if it takes ten containers of popcorn to fill a jar, and each container holds 25 popcorn pieces, then the jar will hold 250 popcorn pieces.

5. Have your child count the number of popcorn pieces in the containers to check his or her estimations.

Parent Letters for the Intermediate Grades ©1997 Creative Teaching Press

Dear Parents,

Did You Know?

When you encourage your child to practice estimation, you are helping him or her get a future job! Many different professionals, such as accountants, chefs, and architects, use estimation to complete their work. By encouraging your child to "estimate before calculate," he or she will strengthen important math skills needed throughout his or her lifetime. The following hands-on activity will help your child "fill in the gaps" as he or she estimates the size and shape of objects.

How You Can Help

1. Have your child estimate the number of marshmallows needed to cover a piece of paper.

2. Invite your child to cover the paper with one layer of marshmallows. Have him or her compare the prediction and results.

3. Discuss possible strategies for making predictions. For example, estimate the number of marshmallows needed to fill one horizontal row and one vertical row and multiply the numbers together.

4. Repeat the process with other items such as pennies, jelly beans, or peanuts. Ask him or her, *Do you think you'll need more or less (the item) to cover the paper? Why?*

5. Ask your child to predict the number of marshmallows (or other items) needed to fill small, rectangular boxes such as a plastic food container or shoe box. Show him or her how to calculate volume *(length x width x height)* to estimate the number of marshmallows needed. Have him or her fill the container to check the prediction.

6. To extend learning, discuss how architects estimate space when designing a house. Invite your child to estimate the area of your living room by using his or her feet, walking heal to toe, to measure length and width. For example, if your child takes 30 steps to walk the length of the room and 20 for the width, the estimated area of the room would be 30 x 20, or 600 square feet.

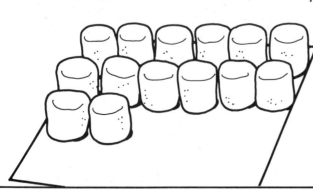

Parent Letters for the Intermediate Grades ©1997 Creative Teaching Press

Dear Parents,

Did You Know?

Estimation and mental math go hand in hand. In order to think through and solve problems quickly, children need to estimate or "approximate" answers. When time is short or information limited, the ability to estimate will help your child determine reasonable solutions to problems. The following interactive game will show your child how estimation can be used to predict final outcomes.

How You Can Help

1. Four players are needed to play this game. You'll need a bowl of pennies (or beans), four different markers (colored chips, stickers, buttons), and paper and pencil.

2. Number the corners of a sheet of paper 0–3, and place a handful of pennies in the center.

3. Invite players to predict the number of pennies left over after the "money pot" is evenly distributed. Have each player place a marker beside the corner number that agrees with his or her prediction.

4. Evenly distribute pennies into four piles. Count leftovers and award them to the players with the matching number.

5. Place the pennies back in the bowl and play again. Take turns placing handfuls of pennies in the pot.

6. Whichever player collects the most leftover pennies after ten rounds wins the game.

Dear Parents,

Did You Know?

Estimation involves comparing the "known" with the "unknown." For example, you can estimate the amount of food to prepare for dinner because you know about how much each family member will eat. The ability to compare and contrast is especially important when estimating the size of objects. The following activity will help your child use visual "cues" and prior knowledge to improve the accuracy of estimations.

How You Can Help

1. Give your child yarn (or string) and a pair of scissors.

2. Cross your arms and stand ten feet away from your child. Ask him or her to cut a piece of yarn to match the length of your arm.

3. Uncross your arms and hold one out for your child to see. Invite your child to cut another matching yarn piece.

4. Have your child measure the length of your arm from wrist to shoulder using a third piece of yarn.

5. Have your child check the accuracy of the estimations by comparing the yarn pieces. Discuss whether or not seeing your arm clearly helped him or her estimate.

6. Repeat the process, estimating and measuring different body parts.

7. Invite your child to make a "guess-and-test" display chart by gluing yarn pieces on poster board to show comparisons.

8. To extend learning, invite your child to estimate length in inches or centimeters. Have him or her use measuring tape to determine actual lengths.

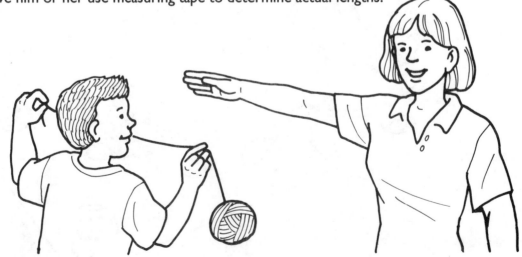

Parent Letters for the Intermediate Grades © 1997 Creative Teaching Press

Dear Parents,

Did You Know?

Estimation skills enable us to calculate problems "on the spot." Many real-life situations require us to think through and solve problems without paper and pencil or calculators. By using mental estimation to determine answers, your child learns valuable and practical math skills. The next time you visit a grocery store or sit down to eat a meal, try the following estimation activities with your child.

How You Can Help

1. The next time you go to the grocery story, invite your child to estimate the weight of different fruits and vegetables. Have him or her check the accuracy of the estimations by weighing the food.

2. Invite your child to estimate the weight of foods using a "hand balance." Have him or her weigh an apple, then use it to gauge the weight of other foods. Ask him or her to weigh the items after estimating weights "by hand."

3. Give your child a slice of fruit such as watermelon or cantaloupe. Have him or her count the number of seeds in the slice, then estimate the total amount in the whole fruit. Invite him or her to check estimations by counting the seeds.

4. Pour a cup of raisin cereal into a bowl. Ask your child to count the number of raisins he or she sees without touching the cereal, then use this "sampling" to estimate how many raisins are in the entire bowl. Invite your child to count raisins and compare the number to his or her estimation.

5. Give your child a clear, plastic bag or jar of mixed nuts. Choose one kind of nut, such as cashew, and have your child count those he or she sees in the unopened bag. Have him or her use this knowledge to estimate the total amount in the entire bag. Invite your child to open the bag and check his or her prediction.

Estimation

Dear Parents,

Did You Know?

Money is a fun, easy way for children to strengthen important math skills. Children are quick to learn the importance of place value when they see $10 magically "change" to $1,000 by moving a decimal point. Having opportunities to add, subtract, multiply, and divide money also shows children the purpose for learning decimals—errors could literally be "costly." Use the following money game to help your child develop winning strategies and "cash in" on his or her math skills.

How You Can Help

1. To play this game, use the attached game sheet, a die, and pencils.

2. Have your child roll the die and write the number on any of the three lines for Check 1.

3. Take your turn rolling the die and writing the number on any of the lines for Check 2.

4. Continue taking turns rolling the die and writing numbers on the remaining lines of Checks 1 and 2. The player with the biggest check wins.

5. Repeat the game using other blank checks. Roll the die as many times as there are blank lines on the check.

6. As an alternative, challenge your child to write the smallest check.

Parent Letters for the Intermediate Grades ©1997 Creative Teaching Press

Blank Check

Check 1

$ __ . __ __

Check 2

$ __ . __ __

Check 3

$ __ __ . __ __

Check 4

$ __ __ . __ __

Check 5

$ __ __ __ . __ __

Check 6

$ __ __ __ . __ __

Check 7

$ __ , __ __ __ . __ __

Check 8

$ __ , __ __ __ . __ __

Decimals and Money

Dear Parents,

Did You Know?

Money is a natural motivator for teaching math—what child doesn't love to spend money? Use money to teach your child important math skills such as adding and subtracting decimals, "greater than/less than" number sense, skip counting (counting by 5s, 10s, 25s, and so on), estimation, and equivalent values (e.g., ten pennies is equivalent to one dime). The following fun, hands-on activity will help your child make "sense" out of money.

How You Can Help

1. Gather a cup of pennies, a handful of dimes, and a die.

2. Invite your child to to roll the die and count out pennies or dimes (one or the other, not a mixture) to match the number rolled. For example, a roll of *five* could equal five dimes or five pennies.

3. Take turns rolling the die and collecting coins. Encourage your child to trade groups of 10 pennies for dimes.

4. The winner is whomever collects *exactly* $1.00 or is closest to $1.00 after five rounds.

5. As a variation, add nickels to the game, or change the target amount to $5.00.

Parent Letters for the Intermediate Grades ©1997 Creative Teaching Press

Dear Parents,

Did You Know?

An easy way to excite and motivate children about word problems is to tie in money skills. Many times children are confused by the vague, abstract language used in story problems—they can't understand or relate to what is written. Children understand and relate to money. Money is meaningful in their lives, and they are eager to use it wisely. Help your child strengthen critical-thinking and problem-solving skills by showing him or her the value of money. Use the following activity to help you get started.

How You Can Help

1. Give your child a "spending allowance," for example, $75.00.

2. Invite your child to "buy" gifts for family members by looking through catalogs.

3. Ask your child to write gifts "purchased" on the attached order form. Have him or her calculate the amount of money remaining after each purchase. For example, if your child buys a gift for $15.00, he or she would have $60.00 left to spend.

4. For an extra challenge, have your child include the cost of sales tax (according to where you live). For example, if your sales tax is 7%, tax on a $15.00 item would be $1.05 (7% x $15.00 = 0.07 x 15.00 = $1.05), therefore, the total cost would be $16.05.

5. As an extension, give your child actual bills and coins to work with as he or she calculates costs.

6. As an alternative, give your child a clothing budget and have him or her use the order form to keep track of purchases.

Item	Quantity	Price	Price with Tax	Money Remaining
Blouse	1	$15.00		

Shopper's Order Form

Name _____   **Phone Number** _____

Address _____

_____

_____

Item	Quantity	Price	Price with Tax	Money Remaining

Parent Letters for the Intermediate Grades ©1997 Creative Teaching Press

Dear Parents,

Did You Know?

You can provide valuable problem-solving practice for your chil
her in various money-related household decisions. It is impor
how different math operations (addition, subtraction, multir
with real-life situations. The following "real-world" math
your child's problem-solving skills.

How You Can Help

1. Take your child to the grocery store to help you choose the best bargains.
   For example, if a three-roll pack of paper towels costs $1.93, ask your child if this
   is better than one roll for 69 cents. Invite your child to take along a calculator to
   help add up the total costs.

2. The next time you go clothes shopping, invite your child to calculate prices of
   discounted items. For example, 10% off $10.00 would mean a discount price of
   $9.00 (10% of $10.00 = 0.10 x 10.00 = $1.00). Encourage your child to calculate
   answers mentally, or invite him or her to bring along a calculator.

3. Invite your child to calculate the expenses for a one-week trip to a "dream"
   destination. Have your child use newspaper listings to determine the costs for
   food, clothing, transportation, hotel accomodations, and entertainment. To extend
   learning, invite him or her to map out the trip and read travel guides to learn more
   about the region.

4. Invite your child to measure the dimensions of his or her room and plan new uses
   for wall, closet, and floor space. If "redecorating" includes the purchase of new
   items, have him or her "shop around" to look for the best bargains, then calculate
   the overall costs.

5. For an extra challenge, have your child devise an imaginary monthly budget for
   overall living expenses. Give him or her "money" to last for one month. Ask him
   or her to budget money for food, clothing, housing, transportation, and entertainment. Invite your child to keep a record of daily expenses, then calculate the total
   costs at the end of the month to see if the budget was maintained.

Decimals and Money

Dear Parents,

Did You Know?

Your child will be more successful understanding and calculating fractions if he or she divides actual objects into halves, fourths, thirds, and other fractional parts. Children at all levels of math benefit from using manipulatives—objects that help them "see" math problems. Have your child experience fractions "naturally" by completing the following hands-on activities at home.

How You Can Help

1. Help your child prepare a fruit salad for dinner by cutting various fruits into halves, fourths, and eighths. Compare and discuss the sizes of different fractional pieces. Invite your child to cut and compare other fractional pieces such as thirds, sixths, and twelfths.

2. The next time you serve food such as pizza, waffles, or brownies, invite your child to learn about fractions while serving others. Have your child cut the food, then compare the cut portions to the fractions they represent. For example, *When you cut a pizza into eight equal-sized slices, that means eight people each receive 1/8 of the pizza.*

3. Explore other fractions, using measuring cups and various liquids—water, milk, and syrup. For added fun, have your child practice fractions while helping you cook special recipes.

Dear Parents,

Did You Know?

Part of understanding fractions is realizing they are numbers that can be ordered, added, subtracted, multiplied, and divided. Before children can calculate with fractions in writing, they need to see the process using paper pieces and/or illustrations. Help your child "piece together" his or her knowledge of fractions by playing the following fun, interactive game.

How You Can Help

1. Cover a die with tape and label sides *1/16, 1/16, 1/8, 1/8, 1/4,* and *1/2*.

2. Have your child cut apart the attached fraction pieces—one set for each player.

3. Have each player place two half pieces on top of the "whole" strip.

4. Take turns rolling the die and removing corresponding fraction pieces from the strip. To do so, players may need to exchange pieces. For example, if a player rolls 1/4, he or she could exchange one half for one 1/4 and two 1/8s, then remove 1/4 from his or her strip.

5. Have each player roll the die only once during his or her turn. If he or she does not have the correct fractional piece to exchange, the game moves on to the next player.

6. The first player to completely uncover his or her paper strip wins.

Parent Letters for the Intermediate Grades ©1997 Creative Teaching Press

Fraction Exchange

1 Whole

1/2	1/2

1/4	1/4	1/4	1/4

1/8	1/8	1/8	1/8	1/8	1/8	1/8	1/8

1/16	1/16	1/16	1/16	1/16	1/16	1/16	1/16	1/16	1/16	1/16	1/16	1/16	1/16	1/16	1/16

1 Whole

1/2	1/2

1/4	1/4	1/4	1/4

1/8	1/8	1/8	1/8	1/8	1/8	1/8	1/8

1/16	1/16	1/16	1/16	1/16	1/16	1/16	1/16	1/16	1/16	1/16	1/16	1/16	1/16	1/16	1/16

Parent Letters for the Intermediate Grades ©1997 Creative Teaching Press

Dear Parents,

Did You Know?

Children learn best when they interact with concrete objects. This is especially true for geometry—the branch of mathematics dealing with shapes, solid objects, and positions in space (points and lines). Rather than having your child memorize definitions and terms, help him or her experience geometry through puzzles, games, and art projects. The following activity will help you "shape up" your child's knowledge of geometry.

How You Can Help

1. Glue the attached tangram square to poster board.

2. Have your child cut along the lines to make seven geometric pieces—five triangles, a square, and a parallelogram.

3. Invite your child to explore the pieces, putting them together to create various shapes.

4. Ask your child to reassemble pieces into a square using a few or all pieces. Encourage him or her to discover more than one solution.

5. Challenge your child to use tangram pieces to build the shapes illustrated below. For extra fun, invite him or her to make new designs.

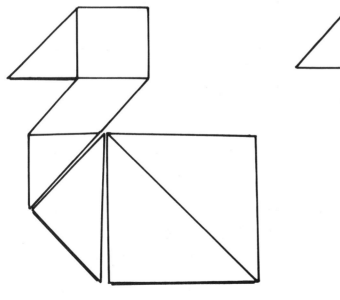
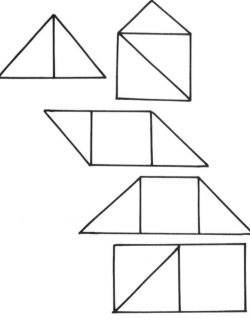

Tangrams

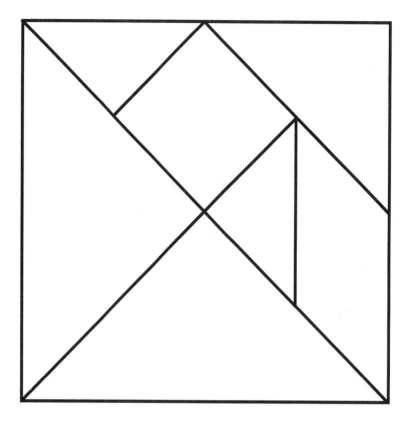

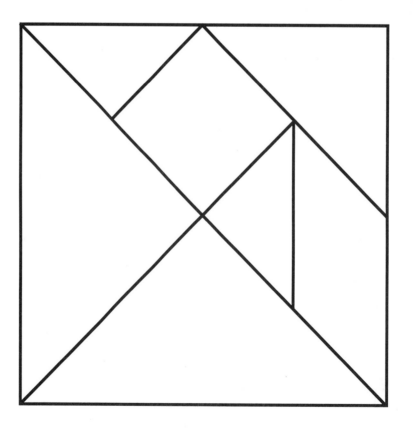

Parent Letters for the Intermediate Grades ©1997 Creative Teaching Press

Dear Parents,

Did You Know?

Geometry includes both two- and three-dimensional shapes. Most two-dimensional, "flat" shapes are polygons—closed figures that include lines and angles, such as triangles, squares, and rectangles. Circles are two-dimensional, but they are not polygons because they have curves instead of lines and angles. Help your child learn about polygons and other shapes by doing games and activities that involve shapes. The more your child "sees" geometry, the better prepared he or she will be for advanced geometry concepts. Here's one geometric "puzzler" to help you get started.

How You Can Help

1. Draw enlarged polygons (triangle, square, pentagon, diamond, octagon) on poster board. Cut out the shapes, and trace them on white paper to make puzzle "guides."

2. Cut each shape into six pieces. Place puzzles in separate labeled envelopes.

3. Give your child an envelope and have him or her put the pieces together to form the polygon. If your child has difficulty, give him or her the puzzle guide for reference.

4. Repeat with other puzzles.

5. For extra challenge, cut puzzles into smaller pieces, or mix two puzzles together, before giving them to your child.

6. Invite your child to make other polygon puzzles. For extra fun, have him or her cut pieces to match the number of sides in each polygon. For example, the pentagon puzzle would have five pieces since it has five sides.

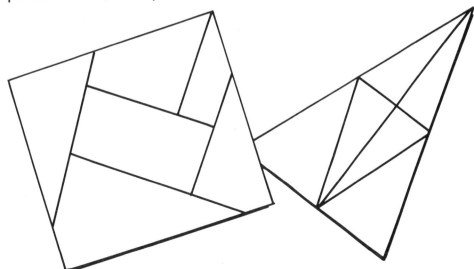

Dear Parents,

Did You Know?

Every time your child looks at real-life objects, he or she is learning geometry. Everything in our world is made of shapes. Some are rounded (circles, ovals, spheres), some have lines and corners (squares, rectangles, triangles), and others are a combination of both. You can help your child learn geometry by looking at shapes in your environment. The following art activities bring the versatility of shapes into view.

How You Can Help

1. Ask your child to identify shapes of objects in and around the home, such as cooking utensils, food containers, hardware supplies, road signs, and building structures.

2. Have your child find shapes in magazine and newspaper pictures. Invite him or her to cut them out to make a shape collage. As an alternative, have your child group cutouts of similar shape. Invite him or her to glue shapes by category on poster board to make a column chart or pictograph.

3. Invite your child to cut out geometric shapes from construction paper and use them to make pictures, such as a boat, car, rocket, flower, or clown. Encourage your child to include the following polygons, labeling each piece.

    triangle (three sides)
    square (four sides, equal in length)
    rectangle (four sides, opposite sides parallel and equal in length)
    trapezoid (four sides, only two of which are parallel)
    pentagon (five sides)
    hexagon (six sides)
    heptagon (seven sides)
    octagon (eight sides)
    nonagon (nine sides)
    decagon (ten sides)

Parent Letters for the Intermediate Grades ©1997 Creative Teaching Press

Dear Parents,

Did You Know?

Three-dimensional objects are those with depth—they "reach out" into space. In geometry, we call 3-D figures with four or more faces (flat surfaces) *polyhedrons*. Each face of a polyhedron is a polygon. There are many different kinds of polyhedrons your child can explore, including pyramids (four faces), triangular prisms (five faces), and cubes (six faces). Use the following model-building activity to add depth to your child's understanding of 3-D geometry.

How You Can Help

1. Give your child plenty of toothpicks and "connectors" (miniature marshmallows, gumdrops, raisins, clay balls).

2. Have him or her use toothpicks and connectors to make the two-dimensional shapes (polygons) shown below. Invite your child to name each shape and count the number of sides and angles.

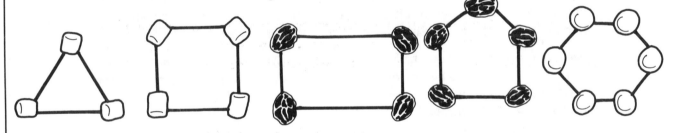

3. Ask your child to make 3-D shapes such as those shown below. Have him or her count the number of lines, angles, and faces. Ask him or her to identify which polygon is formed on the face of each 3-D shape. For example, each side of a cube is a square.

4. Invite your child to make additional 3-D shapes. Encourage him or her to be creative and have fun!

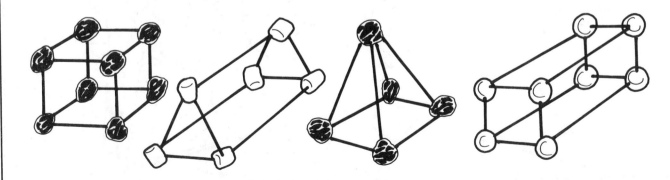

Geometry and Patterns

Dear Parents,

Did You Know?

Most plants and animals are symmetrical. They have a "line of symmetry"—an imaginary line that divides them into "mirror images." For example, humans have a line of symmetry from head to toe, dividing them into two equal halves with similar parts (e.g., eye, ear, arm, leg). Use the following activities to help your child learn more about real-life symmetrical objects.

How You Can Help

1. Invite your child to make symmetrical paper cutouts. Have him or her fold paper in half and cut shapes along the crease. Discuss how the two sides of each shape are symmetrical—mirror images of each other.

2. Have your child identify symmetrical objects found in and around your home, such as road signs, tables, and leaves. Discuss how humans and animals are built symmetrically.

3. Invite your child to cut out a large front-view picture of a person or animal. Have him or her cut the picture in half along the line of symmetry.

4. Ask your child to glue one half of the picture on white construction paper, and discard the rest. Invite him or her to draw the other side, replacing the half that was cut away. Encourage him or her to look at and use "clues" from the cut picture to draw the mirror image.

5. As an extension, have your child look for and compare lines of symmetry in numbers and letters—some have more than one line of symmetry, whereas others have none at all. For example, the letter *X* has two lines of symmetry, whereas the letter *R* has none. Invite your child to discover other objects in and around the home containing more than one line of symmetry.

Parent Letters for the Intermediate Grades ©1997 Creative Teaching Press

Dear Parents,

Did You Know?

The most important part of solving word problems is figuring out *what to do* rather than *how to do it*. Children not only need to know how to add, subtract, multiply, and divide, but also when to apply each operation in problem-solving situations. Help your child become a successful problem solver by using the following simple strategies.

How You Can Help

1. Encourage your child to read, not skim, problems. Remind him or her that word problems require thorough, careful reading to understand the overall situation and determine the course of action.

2. Have your child verbalize the problem, explaining in his or her own words what the problem is about and what kind of information is needed. Discuss possible ways of working out the problem without indicating which method is correct.

3. Invite your child to use objects or sketches to illustrate word problems. Many times, visual images clarify information.

4. Have your child "act out" word problems. Your child will find this approach entertaining and fun, and it will help him or her "see" solutions previously overlooked.

5. Have your child substitute smaller, simpler numbers for larger, more complex ones (fractions, decimals). This will help your child focus on what needs to be done rather than the "scary" numbers being used.

Terry lives 10 miles from school. Mary lives 5 miles further from school. How far away is Mary from school?

Dear Parents,

Did You Know?

Making up word problems and hearing others invent them helps children understand the strong connection between math and the real world. Before your child can successfully solve word problems, he or she needs to understand why it makes sense to add, subtract, multiply, or divide. The following activity will help your child learn the "language" of word problems.

How You Can Help

1. Write operation symbols *(+, −, x, ÷)* and numerals (*1, 2, 3,* and so on) on separate index cards.

2. Choose two number cards and one operation symbol to make a number sentence. For example, 3 x 5.

3. Give your child a real-life example of how to use the number sentence. For example, *Mark, Steve, and Robin have five baseball cards each. How many cards do they have altogether?* The challenge is not to come up with an answer, but to create a situation around the problem.

4. Invite your child and other family members to use number sentences in stories about real-life situations. Have a contest to see who can come up with the silliest number-sentence story.

Parent Letters for the Intermediate Grades ©1997 Creative Teaching Press

Dear Parents,

Did You Know?

Success in math often comes from being able to see problems in a new way. When you encourage your child to look for "hidden" solutions, you help him or her think critically and creatively. Use the following hands-on activity to help your child "take another look" when solving challenging math problems.

How You Can Help

1. Use 17 toothpicks to make the following figure for your child.

2. Ask your child to remove five toothpicks and leave three squares.

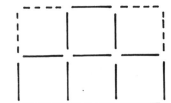

3. Have your child replace all toothpicks, then remove six to show two squares.

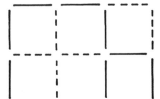

4. Use twelve toothpicks to make the following figure.

5. Ask your child to remove four toothpicks and leave three triangles.

Problem Solving

Dear Parents,

Did You Know?

Children become better problem solvers when encouraged to "experiment" with math. Often there is more than one "right" way to solve a problem. Whether it's calculating math equations or solving real-life situations, encourage your child to examine all options and experiment with possible solutions before making final decisions. Your child will be amazed at how many options there are to choose from!

How You Can Help

1. To play this family game, you'll need a deck of cards, scratch paper, and pencils.

2. Distribute scratch paper and pencils to players. Give each person four cards, and place one card face up in the center of the table.

3. Explain the object of the game—to add, subtract, multiply, and/or divide playing-card numbers to equal the value shown on the table. For example, if the card on the table is six and a player is holding an eight, three, ace (a value of one), and ten: $10 + 3 + 1 - 8 = 6$.

4. Award points for every correct number sentence. Give a bonus point to any player using all four cards.

5. Continue the game by dealing new cards after each round. The first person to score ten points wins the game.

6. For more challenge, have players calculate problems mentally, without using scratch paper.

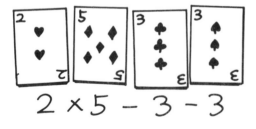

$$2 \times 5 - 3 - 3$$

$$4 + 9 - 3 - 6$$

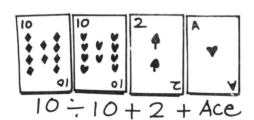

$$10 \div 10 + 2 + Ace$$

Parent Letters for the Intermediate Grades ©1997 Creative Teaching Press

Dear Parents,

Did You Know?

Children need to talk about math. They need to understand that math is more than manipulating numbers—it's a way of thinking. By encouraging your child to "talk it out," you help him or her clarify math concepts and learn from others' ideas. Try the following creative approach to help your child think and talk about math.

How You Can Help

1. Every morning, surprise your child with a "math stumper." Write a problem on a piece of paper, then attach it to his or her pillow, the bathroom mirror, a pair of shoes, or any other item your child encounters as he or she prepares for school.

2. Choose challenging, real-life situations as stumpers. For example, *Yesterday I had $15.00 to buy groceries, but the food plus tax totaled $17.50. In my grocery cart, I had a bag of apples at $2.35, a loaf a bread at $1.89, a jar of peanut butter at $3.25, a package of chicken at $4.50, a gallon of milk at $3.00, and a bag of candy at $1.25. What do you think I did?*

3. During breakfast or dinner, invite your child to share the math stumper with other family members.

4. Explore and discuss together different ways to solve the stumpers. Encourage your child to be thoughtful and creative in his or her answers.

5. Extend the activity by inviting your child to write math stumpers for others family members to solve.

Dear Parents,

Did You Know?

Good mathematicians experiment with different approaches and learn from their mistakes. When mistakes and confusion are accepted as part of the learning process, children develop persistence in solving problems. The following game is a fun mental challenge that encourages your child to "try, try again."

How You Can Help

1. To play this game, you need the attached game sheet, scratch paper, and a pencil.

2. Think of a two-digit number, write it on scratch paper, and turn it face down on the table.

3. Invite your child to try to identify the number you've written on the paper. Ask him or her to write guesses one at a time on the game sheet. He or she will need to look at "clues" you provide to make thoughtful, educated guesses.

   ● Write an X in the "Hey" column if your child has one correct digit, but in the wrong position.

   ● Write an X in the "Yea" column if he or she has one correct digit in the correct position.

   ● Write and X in the "Nay" column if your child has nothing correct.

4. Encourage your child to review and compare all clues after each guess. Continue the process until he or she guesses the correct number.

5. If your child is still stumped by the fifteenth try, reveal the secret number. Go over each clue and discuss the strategies used.

6. Have your child "mentally replay" the sequence of clues using the actual number. This will help him or her see more clearly the connections between the clues and the number.

7. Switch roles and invite your child to select a secret number and provide the clues.

Parent Letters for the Intermediate Grades ©1997 Creative Teaching Press

Hey, Yea, Nay

	GUESS	HEY Correct digit, wrong position	YEA Correct digit, correct position	NAY Nothing correct
1				
2				
3				
4				
5				
6				
7				
8				
9				
10				
11				
12				
13				
14				
15				

Problem Solving

Dear Parents,

Did You Know?

Puzzles and games are not only fun, but also help children learn math! When children solve puzzles and play games, they practice basic math skills (addition, subtraction, multiplication, division), develop "number sense," and use problem-solving strategies. Public libraries and children's bookstores are excellent places to look for fun math activities to play with your child. The following game helps your child develop a "taste" for math.

How You Can Help

1. Place 21 M&Ms (or peanuts) in the center of the table.

2. Take turns removing one or two candies from the pile.

3. The player who gets his or her opponent to remove the last piece from the pile wins all the candy.

4. Play again and invite other family members to join the fun.

5. As a variation, use 50 candies instead of 21. Take turns removing one to six pieces at a time.

Parent Letters for the Intermediate Grades ©1997 Creative Teaching Press

Dear Parents,

Did You Know?

Mental math games not only strengthen important math skills, but also encourage children to search for patterns and relationships that may have been overlooked. Children are more motivated to think through and examine information carefully when trying to win a game. Watch your child have fun planning winning strategies as you play the following mental math game together.

How You Can Help

1. To play this game, you need the attached Sink or Swim game sheet, one pair of dice, and two fish crackers.

2. You and your child each place a cracker on the word *start*.

3. Ask your child to roll the dice and mentally add, subtract, multiply, or divide the two numbers. If the answer is an odd number, he or she moves his or her fish one space toward the shark. If the answer is an even number, he or she moves the fish toward the life raft.

4. Take turns rolling the dice and moving fish on the game board.

5. Whoever reaches the life raft first earns five points. If a player reaches the shark first, he or she earns two points.

6. Play as many games as you can in ten minutes. The player with the most points wins the game.

7. To make the game more challenging, use stickers to replace numbers on the dice with more "complex" digits (two-digit numbers, decimals).

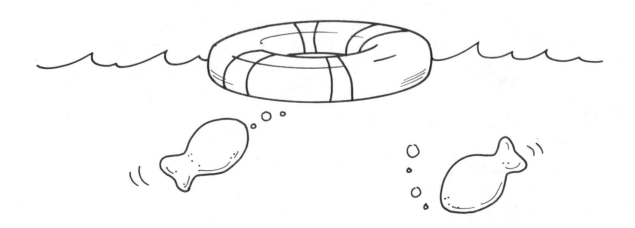

Problem Solving

Sink or Swim

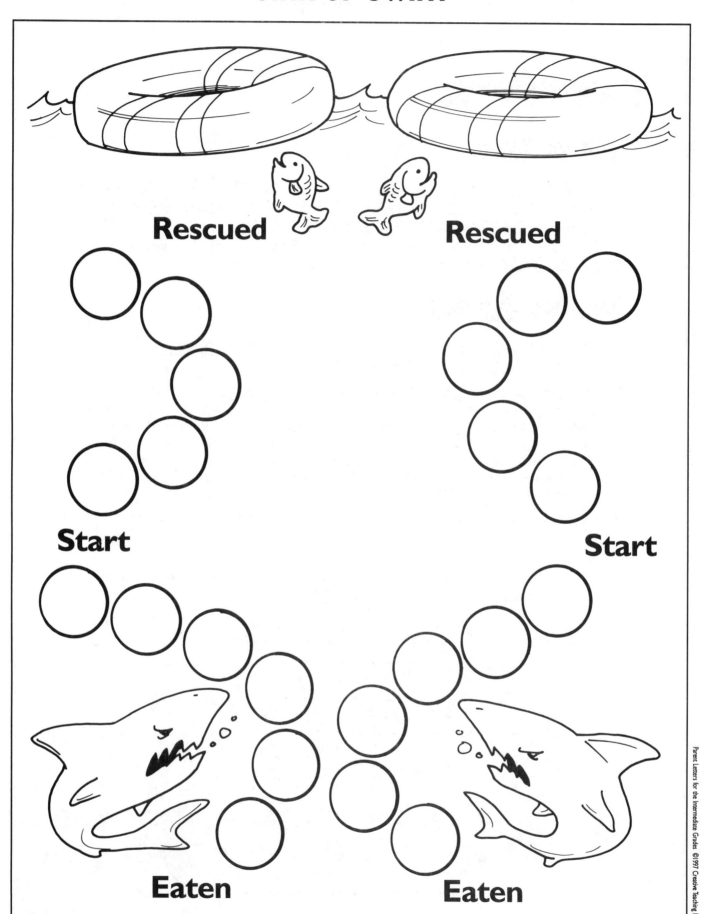

Rescued

Rescued

Start

Start

Eaten

Eaten

Parent Letters for the Intermediate Grades ©1997 Creative Teaching Press

Dear Parents,

Did You Know?

Playing games is a fun way to strengthen basic math skills (adding, subtracting, multiplying, dividing) as well as teach your child how to plan winning strategies. When your child plans and performs game strategies, he or she uses critical thinking to connect basic skills to complex situations. The following version of Tic-Tac-Toe will help your child move beyond drill and practice into fun, exciting math learning.

How You Can Help

1. Draw a game board as shown. Give yourself and your child different sets of markers—beans, cereal pieces, buttons, or pennies.

2. Have your child place two paper clips on numbers in the top row (numbers *1–9*), then multiply these numbers and place a marker on the answer in the grid. For example, if your child places paper clips on numbers *3* and *7*, he or she would cover *21* with a marker.

3. Take your turn by moving one of the paper clips to another number in the row and repeating the process.

4. Continue taking turns until one player gets four markers in a horizontal, vertical, or diagonal row.

| 1 | 2 | 3 | 4 | 5 | 6 | 7 | 8 | 9 |

1	2	3	4	5	6
7	8	9	10	12	14
15	16	18	20	21	24
25	27	28	30	32	35
36	40	42	45	48	49
54	56	63	64	72	81

Problem Solving

Dear Parents,

Did You Know?

Puzzles are a great way to get children to "think math." When children solve math puzzles, they not only practice basic number facts, but also develop "number sense" and problem-solving strategies. The following fun-to-solve puzzles encourage your child to think in mathematical and scientific ways.

How You Can Help

1. Draw a vertical line on separate index cards. Label cards *Magic Line A, Magic Line B, Magic Line C,* and so on. Draw a box at the bottom of each card to record predictions.

2. Secretly decide which math function each line will perform, then fill in numbers to fit the pattern. For example, to show a line that "magically" doubles numbers, write numbers *2, 3,* and *4* on the left side of the line, and numbers *4, 6,* and *8* on the right.

3. Help your child compare numbers on the left of the "magic" line to those on the right. Invite him or her to guess the rule for each card and write a prediction in the box.

4. Share and discuss the correct solutions with your child.

5. Repeat with new magic cards.

6. For an extra challenge, leave off some numbers and have your child "fill in the blanks" by determining the number pattern.

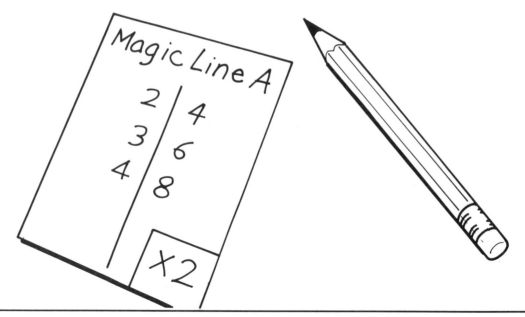

Parent Letters for the Intermediate Grades © 1997 Creative Teaching Press

Dear Parents,

Did You Know?

In science, "communication" means more than talking to others. It includes organizing and writing down observations in ways others can understand—accurate pictures, diagrams, maps, charts, graphs, models, and exhibits. Help your child learn these communication skills by encouraging him or her to evaluate and discuss what he or she says or does. Your own backyard is an excellent arena for developing both observation and communication skills. Use the following tree activity to help your child's scientific skills "grow."

How You Can Help

1. Invite your child to periodically observe a favorite tree over the next few months (ideally, for a 12-month period). Ask him or her to record all observations in a "tree journal."

2. Invite your child to determine the approximate age of the tree by measuring the circumference of its trunk. For example, trees grow about one inch a year, so a tree with a 40" circumference would be approximately 40 years old.

3. Have your child note changes in the leaves and bark of the tree. Invite him or her to draw pictures or take photographs of the tree every few weeks.

4. Invite your child to add leaf and bark rubbings to the journal. Place a sheet of paper over a leaf or section of bark, then rub a crayon over the paper to make the rubbings.

5. Invite your child to add leaf pressings to his or her journal. Place the leaves between several sheets of newspaper, then press dry by covering them with heavy objects for three weeks.

6. Encourage your child to discover ways his or her tree provides food and shelter for people and animals. If the tree has fruit, invite your child to make special treats with the fruit for family members.

7. Use notes and pictures in the journal to compare and discuss with your child changes in his or her tree from the beginning of the observation period to the end.

Dear Parents,

Did You Know?

When we make conclusions based on indirect evidence or clues, it is called "inference." For example, when we see someone laugh, we may infer he or she is amused. Scientists often rely on inference when direct evidence is impossible to obtain. For example, scientists have never visited the center of the earth, but are able to infer much about its properties. Your child, too, will need to rely on inference when making decisions, scientific or otherwise. Help strengthen your child's ability to infer and draw conclusions by performing scientific explorations like the following.

How You Can Help

1. Have your child gather ten food items such as salami, milk, peanut butter, potato chips, butter, celery, apples, and chocolate to test for fat.

2. Ask your child to rub each food on a separate paper square. Have him or her use a clean spoon to dab and rub on soft or liquid foods, wiping off any excess.

3. Let the paper squares dry. Ask your to child hold each paper up to a light. Have him or her infer which foods contain fat by looking for paper squares with grease marks.

4. Invite your child to test the same foods for the presence of carbohydrates (starch). Have him or her place a drop of iodine on the food—if there's starch present, the food will turn a blue-black color.

Parent Letters for the Intermediate Grades ©1997 Creative Teaching Press

Dear Parents,

Did You Know?

Asking open-ended questions encourages children to think carefully, creatively, and independently about science. Open-ended questions are those that begin with such words as *How can you . . . ? What will happen if . . . ? What conditions are best for . . . ?* and *What else could be done to . . . ?* You can help your child improve important science skills by asking him or her broad questions while exploring everyday objects and events. Use the following outdoor activity to help you get started.

How You Can Help

1. The next time you spot a colony of ants at a family picnic, invite your child to observe and describe what he or she sees.

2. Ask your child open-ended questions such as:
   ● *What do you think would happen if you place a piece of food near the ants?*
   ● *What do you think would happen if you place the food farther away?*
   ● *What do you think would happen if you give covered food to the ants?*
   ● *How do you think ants know where to look for food?*

3. Invite your child to conduct "tests" to answer these questions. First, have him or her place a piece of food near the ant colony and see what happens. Have your child look for signs of teamwork and communication—ants carrying food together, touching antennae, and leading others down a trail.

4. Next, have your child move the food farther away from the colony and compare the results. Ask specific, "narrow" questions such as *How many ants discovered the food first? What do the "discoverers" do once they find the food—do they leave it behind to tell others, carry it back to the ant hill, or eat the food on the spot?*

5. Last, ask your child to cover another piece of food with a napkin and place it near the ant colony. Have your child observe what happens. Ask questions such as *Which food do you think was easier for the ants to find—covered or uncovered? How do you know? How do you think ants find hidden food? Do you think ants can smell? What other ways could ants detect food without seeing or smelling?*

Life Science

Dear Parents,

Did You Know?

You can teach your child about proper health and nutrition right in your own kitchen! When your child looks at nutritional facts on food labels and monitors what your family eats, he or she learns to make better food choices. Try the following "food-for-thought" activities to help your child become more health conscious.

How You Can Help

1. Have your child fill out the attached refrigerator inventory. Ask him or her to list the names of foods in your refrigerator that fit under each category.

2. Ask your child to tally the foods eaten for one day. Have him or her compare tallies to the recommended daily servings shown below. Discuss whether or not he or she is eating a healthy, balanced diet.

3. Invite your child and other family members to look at nutritional fact sheets from various fast-food restaurants. Compare the amounts of fat, sugar, carbohydrates, and protein in different foods.

4. Invite your child to help prepare healthy, nutritious meals for the family. Encourage him or her to include foods from each major food group.

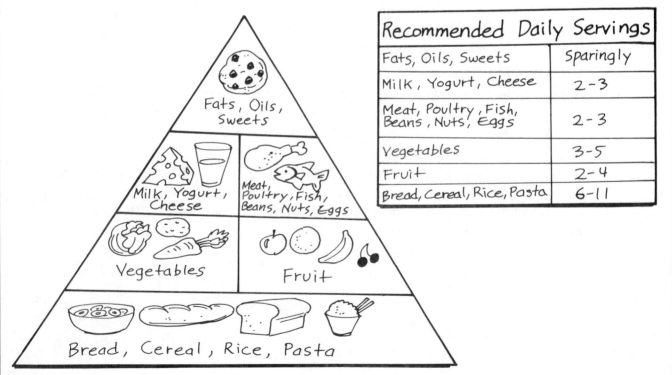

Recommended Daily Servings	
Fats, Oils, Sweets	Sparingly
Milk, Yogurt, Cheese	2-3
Meat, Poultry, Fish, Beans, Nuts, Eggs	2-3
Vegetables	3-5
Fruit	2-4
Bread, Cereal, Rice, Pasta	6-11

Parent Letters for the Intermediate Grades © 1997 Creative Teaching Press

Refrigerator Inventory

Breads, Rice, Cereals, Pasta	Vegetables	Fruits	Milk, Cheese, Yogurt	Meat, Fish, Poultry, Nuts, Eggs, Dried Beans	Fats, Oils, Sweets

Daily Tally

Breads, Rice, Cereals, Pasta	Vegetables	Fruits	Milk, Cheese, Yogurt	Meat, Fish, Poultry, Nuts, Eggs, Dried Beans	Fats, Oils, Sweets

Life Science

Dear Parents,

Did You Know?

Nature explorations provide fun opportunities to practice important science skills. When children are encouraged to discover and share nature, they learn to observe, evaluate, and communicate carefully and completely. The next time your family goes on an outdoor adventure, use the following activity to help your child examine and appreciate the beauty of nature.

How You Can Help

1. Have your child and other family members go on a scavenger hunt in a park or other wooded area. Write a list of items for each "hunter" to find and place in a bag, including:

    - five different kinds of seeds
    - something soft or fuzzy
    - four different kinds of leaves
    - three different kinds of bird food

    - a piece of tree bark
    - something colorful
    - three different kinds of flowers
    - something that makes noise

2. Have family members share their findings. Invite your child to compare the following features.

    - Edges of leaves—Are they smooth, jagged, or lobbed?
    - Vein patterns of leaves—Are they feather-like in pattern (pinnate), or do they contain several main veins of similar size (palmate)?
    - Color and odor of flowers—Which flowers would attract more animals? Why?
    - Flower parts—How many petals, pistils, and stamen in each flower?
    - Seeds—How does each seed travel to a new location?

3. Invite your child to make a 3-D nature book using items found on the scavenger hunt. Have him or her draw or take pictures of "parent" plants, then glue corresponding items found next to each portrait. (Leaves and flowers should be pressed between sheets of newspaper and books for several days before gluing them in the nature book.)

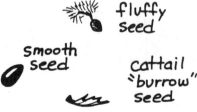

Parent Letters for the Intermediate Grades © 1997 Creative Teaching Press

Dear Parents,

Did You Know?

Nature provides it's own game of Hide and Seek! Many animals protect themselves through camouflage, blending in with the colors and shapes in their environment. Predators must look long and hard to track down these hidden animals. Help your child strengthen critical-observation skills and develop a "predator's eye" by completing hide-and-seek activities like the following.

How You Can Help

1. Hide 10 to 15 man-made objects in your backyard or along a long wooded trail. Include a few bright objects that will "stand out," such as an orange ball or a yellow pail. Other items should blend into their surroundings.

2. Invite family members to walk around the area to spot camouflaged objects. Set a time limit of five minutes. "Explorers" should look, not touch, and keep discoveries a secret.

3. Have your child and other family members share their discoveries. Discuss how some objects were easy to spot due to color or shape, while others were more concealed.

4. Discuss how animals blend into their environment to hide from enemies. Invite your child to look for camouflaged insects in the area.

Life Science

Dear Parents,

Did You Know?

Scientists are similar to detectives. They make decisions based on "evidence"—observations and data collected through tests and experiments. Help your child be a good scientist by encouraging him or her to look for "clues" when solving problems in and around the home. The following fun, hands-on activity will help your child unravel the mysteries of science.

How You Can Help

1. Ask family members to make fingerprints for your child's "record file." Have each person press each finger, one at a time, on a stamp pad and then on white paper.

2. Choose one family member to make fingerprints on a glass while your child is out of the room.

3. Invite your child to determine whose fingerprints are on the glass by "dusting for evidence." Have him or her use baby powder to dust the surface of the glass, carefully blowing off the excess powder to see fingerprints.

4. Ask your child to place a piece of clear, wide tape over the print and gently smooth out the tape to remove air bubbles. Have him or her pull off the tape and stick it to black paper.

5. Ask your child to compare the fingerprint to those "on file." Invite your child to identify who made the prints on the glass.

Parent Letters for the Intermediate Grades ©1997 Creative Teaching Press

Dear Parents,

Did You Know?

Many children rely on sight to make observations and conclusions about their environment. But science involves more than just vision. Important scientific information is also acquired through hearing, smelling, feeling, and tasting. Children should be encouraged to use all their senses when making observations and collecting facts. Try the following activity to help your child "sense" everyday objects and events in a whole new way.

How You Can Help

1. Take your child outdoors to choose a distant destination such as a trash can on the other side of the yard.

2. Blindfold your child and give him or her a ball of string. Invite your child to walk to the chosen destination (trash can), stopping when he or she thinks it's within reach. Follow your child silently, removing any obstructions.

3. Remove the blindfold and let your child see the string path created. Invite your child to describe the experience. Ask how loss of sight affected the ability to "sense" the correct direction.

4. Invite your child to try the test again, this time listening to your voice as you stand next to the "target." Have your child compare the experiences.

5. Encourage your child to observe the environment using all senses—seeing, hearing, smelling, touching, and tasting (when appropriate). Invite him or her to share findings aloud or in writing.

Life Science

Dear Parents,

Did You Know?

When children measure objects, they improve their observation skills. They observe and compare such things as length, width, height, and weight. Scientists rely on measurement to analyze and understand many natural phenomena. For example, measuring shadows at different times of day throughout the year helps scientists understand how the earth revolves around the sun. Encourage your child to do a "shadow study" by completing the following hands-on activity.

How You Can Help

1. Ask your child to stand in a sunny spot while you place a piece of tape at both ends of his or her shadow.

2. Have your child use a tape measure to determine the length of his or her shadow.

3. Ask your child to determine the "shadow number" by measuring his or her actual height and comparing it to that of the shadow. For example, if your child is 50" tall and his or her shadow is 75" long, the "shadow number" is 1.5 since the shadow is 1.5 times longer than his or her actual height (75 ÷ 50 =1.5).

4. Have your child use the "shadow number" to determine the height of tall objects such as a tree, flag pole, or telephone pole. For example, if a tree's shadow measures 60 feet, the tree is approximately 40 feet tall since 60 ÷ 1.5 = 40.

5. Invite your child to calculate and use the "shadow number" at different times throughout the day. He or she will discover that the value changes, but the actual height of objects do not. For example, a morning "test" may show your child's shadow measuring 100" which would lead to a value of 2 (100 ÷ 50 = 2). However, the tree's shadow would also increase proportionately from 60 feet to 80 feet, keeping the actual measurement at 40 (80 ÷ 2 = 40).

Parent Letters for the Intermediate Grades ©1997 Creative Teaching Press

Dear Parents,

Did You Know?

"Open-ended" discoveries encourage divergent thinking—studying a problem or situation from different perspectives. When children have the opportunity to think and explore freely, they are more likely to look for hidden details and new approaches when problem-solving. Help your child "think science" by doing the following open-ended, hands-on exploration.

How You Can Help

1. Give your child an assortment of containers (paper cups, plastic bowls) various food wraps (plastic, tin foil, waxed paper, cellophane), dark and light paper, masking tape, scissors, and water.

2. Invite him or her to use any of the supplies provided to make a homemade solar energy trapper—a container that traps heat from the sun.

3. Have your child place a cup of water in the trapper, set it outside in the sun for one hour, then feel the water to see if it heated.

4. Encourage your child to make and test different models by lining the container with tin foil, covering the container with a "lid," and wrapping the solar heater with dark paper.

5. Invite your child to compare and share results.

6. To extend learning, have your child measure the amount of heat absorbed by placing a thermometer in the water before placing the cup in the solar heater.

7. Discuss how "trapped" solar energy is used in the real world, for example, to heat houses, produce electricity, or cook food.

Earth Science

Dear Parents,

Did You Know?

Some of the best discoveries and inventions have been made through "trial and error." Science often involves trying different approaches and making many mistakes before finding workable solutions. Children should understand that success in science means patience, persistence, and learning from failure. The following Earth-awareness activity will show your child how creativity and perseverance can lead to beneficial results.

How You Can Help

1. For this activity, you'll need a large shallow pan half full of water, salad oil, and various "cleaning supplies" (paper towel, sponge, detergent, craft stick, sand, straw, feather, cotton balls).

2. Have your child pour two tablespoons of oil into the water. Point out how the oil floats to the surface.

3. Explain the damage caused by oil spills. For example, water birds and fish covered with oil die from either toxic effects or the inability to swim. Discuss the importance of keeping water supplies clean for both animals and people.

4. Invite your child to discover the most effective method for cleaning an oil spill. Have him or her try one cleaning material at a time, noting both the material's effect on the oil and visa versa. Then, have your child try a combination of one or more materials to see if the oil can be removed more efficiently.

5. To extend learning, discuss the effects of air pollution on plants and animals. Invite your child to test for air pollution by spreading thin layers of petroleum jelly on plastic milk-jug strips and hanging them in various locations for one week. Have your child check the strips for adhering particles and discuss possible sources for these contaminants.

6. For extra enrichment, invite your child to brainstorm ways to keep water and air clean. Have him or her list ways people can reduce the amount of pollutants released in the environment.

Parent Letters for the Intermediate Grades ©1997 Creative Teaching Press

Dear Parents,

Did You Know?

A glass of water can "open the door" to a world of scientific discoveries! Water is the center of existence for all living things. When your child explores how water is collected, used, and conserved, he or she learns lessons that extend into all areas of science—earth, life, and physical. Help your child "dive" into new discoveries by completing the following water activities together.

How You Can Help

1. Invite your child to list ways he or she uses water, such as for drinking, cleaning dishes, and watering the lawn. Discuss the difficulty of obtaining clean, fresh water. Over 97% of water on Earth is salt water, and 2% is glacier ice. Explain that even though some salt water is "transformed" naturally into fresh water, it is difficult and costly for humans to duplicate the process.

2. Invite your child to extract fresh water from salt water by making a distillation system. Ask him or her to pour 1/2 cup salt water into a large bowl, then place a smaller bowl inside. (Place a rock in the smaller bowl to weigh it down.) Have your child loosely cover the large bowl with plastic wrap, and tape the edges to make it air tight. Ask him or her to place a small pebble or marble in the center of the plastic wrap, creating a cone-shaped indentation. Let the distiller sit undisturbed in a sunny spot for several days.

3. Invite your child to observe the water collecting on the plastic wrap and in the small bowl. Have him or her remove the wrap, and compare the taste of the water in both bowls.

4. Invite your child to explain how the "fresh" water got into the small bowl. Explain that the salt water was purified through the water cycle—the sun caused the water to evaporate, leaving behind the salt; the water "vapor" then condensed on the plastic wrap and dropped into the small bowl.

5. Encourage your child to research and discover more about the water cycle and ways to purify water. To extend learning, invite your child to list ways family members can conserve water in and around the home.

Dear Parents,

Did You Know?

Science involves discovering and establishing "proof." When your child conducts scientific tests and experiments, he or she gathers facts to prove or disprove opinions or beliefs. The next time your child wonders about everyday objects or events, encourage him or her to predict (hypothesize) what will happen, then look for ways to prove the predictions are correct. Use the following activity to help you get started.

How You Can Help

1. Have your child make a glass of salt water by mixing 1/4 cup salt with 1/2 glass of water. Ask him or her to fill a second glass half full with water only.

2. Invite your child to predict what will happen when an uncooked egg is placed in each glass.

3. Ask your child to place an egg in each glass and observe what happens. (The egg in the salt water floats.)

4. Have him or her discuss possible reasons for the results, then provide the answer. (The salt water is more dense than the egg, so the egg floats. The egg is heavier than fresh water, so it sinks to the bottom of the glass.)

5. Discuss how objects float more easily in the ocean. Have your child compare test results to this natural phenomenon. (Salt water is more dense than fresh water, making it easier for heavy objects to float.)

6. Invite your child to repeat testing, using sugar instead of salt, or hard-boiled eggs instead of uncooked eggs. Are the results the same?

Parent Letters for the Intermediate Grades ©1997 Creative Teaching Press

Dear Parents,

Did You Know?

TV weather reports help teach children science. Not only do meteorologists explain weather information in an entertaining way, but they also model important thinking and problem-solving skills. By encouraging your child to "track" the weather, you help him or her learn how to observe, compare, communicate, infer, and apply scientific information. Use the following activity to help your child become a top-notch weather reporter.

How You Can Help

1. Watch a TV weather report with your child. Discuss different problem-solving strategies used by the meteorologist—evaluating his or her previous forecast, studying a weather map, and analyzing weather patterns to predict the next day's weather.

2. Invite your child to predict the weather. Help him or her study and compare newspaper weather maps over several days. Have your child investigate information such as different temperatures across the country and where storm areas are located. Point out how storm fronts generally move from the Pacific Ocean across to the Atlantic Ocean. (They travel about 500 miles a day in the summer and 700 miles a day in the winter.)

3. Have your child record and compare weather predictions to actual weather conditions. Have him or her label one column *Predicted Weather* and another *Actual Weather*. Invite your child to use weather pictures (sun, clouds, snowflakes) to illustrate weather reports.

4. Invite your child to give "weather reports" to family members. Have him or her compare predictions with those on TV and in newspapers.

Earth Science

Dear Parents,

Did You Know?

Nature is science in action! Weather can produce amazing "shows" that teach children about science in the real world. By taking time to watch and study the effects of various weather conditions, your child will learn to observe, compare, infer, and communicate scientific information. The next time you're stuck at home during stormy weather, try this activity to bring a sunny smile to your child's face.

How You Can Help

1. Have your child count the number of seconds between the time he or she sees lightning and hears thunder.

2. Ask your child to use this time value to calculate the approximate distance to the storm. Since sound travels about 1/5 mile per second, divide the seconds counted by five to determine the distance to the storm in miles. For example, if your child counts ten seconds between seeing lightning and hearing thunder, the storm is approximately two miles away (10 ÷ 5 = 2).

3. Ask your child to take several "readings" within a ten-minute period. Have him or her compare readings to decide whether the storm is moving closer or farther away.

4. Encourage your child to read and research interesting facts about thunder and lightning. Invite him or her to find the answers to questions such as:

   ● *How is thunder and lightning produced?*
   ● *Why do we see lightning before hearing thunder?*
   ● *How are lightning and electricity related?*
   ● *What are some dangers of being in a thunderstorm?*

Parent Letters for the Intermediate Grades ©1997 Creative Teaching Press

Dear Parents,

Did You Know?

Young children are natural scientists, fascinated by the world around them and eager to explore its mysteries. Without proper support, however, this interest can deteriorate as children get older. You can help your child maintain excitement and curiosity for science by simply joining in the fun. Collect and perform an assortment of science "tricks" to surprise and amuse your child. The following activity will help you get started.

How You Can Help

1. Have your child place a mixture of salt and pepper on a piece of paper.

2. Give your child a "magic" comb to pass through his or her hair.

3. Tell your child to move the comb close to the salt and pepper, and say the "magic words." He or she will be amazed to see the pepper magically "jump" to the comb.

4. Invite your child to discuss possible reasons why this "trick" happens. (The comb becomes negatively charged when passed through hair, giving it the power to "pick up" light objects. Since pepper is lighter than salt, it is attracted to the comb.)

5. Invite your child to discover other materials attracted to the charged comb. Have him or her test items such as an inflated balloon, plastic wrap, and confetti. Encourage your child to predict which items will "stick" to the comb and which will not.

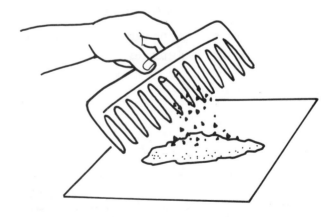

Physical Science

Dear Parents,

Did You Know?

Children who are curious and aware of their surroundings have greater success in science. They use their senses (sight, smell, taste, touch, hearing) to observe and compare similarities and differences between objects and events. Help your child strengthen observation skills right in your own home. A great place to start is the kitchen—it's filled with simple, ready-to-use supplies to "cook up" scientific discoveries.

How You Can Help

1. In advance, place small amounts of salt, sugar, cornstarch, and baking soda on separate index cards labeled *A, B, C,* and *D*. Make a note of which letter corresponds to which ingredient. Keep the identity of these "mystery powders" secret from your child.

2. Place additional samples of salt, sugar, cornstarch, and baking soda on waxed-paper pieces. Identify the samples, and invite your child to look at, smell, touch, and taste each one. If possible, provide him or her with a magnifying glass for a closer look. Ask your child to write down his or her observations.

3. Have your child use an eyedropper to add water to each sample. Ask him or her to observe and record what happens. Repeat the process using vinegar, then iodine. Ask your child to record observations after each step.

4. Give your child the "mystery powders." Invite him or her to guess the identity of each one by adding water, vinegar, and iodine. Encourage your child to refer to his or her notes before making final decisions.

5. Reveal the identity of the powders. Discuss how testing and observing the "known" samples helped solve the mystery.

6. For a more challenging experiment, use "mystery powders" that are a combination of two or three substances.

Parent Letters for the Intermediate Grades ©1997 Creative Teaching Press

Dear Parents,

Did You Know?

To nurture scientific discovery, children need to explore the physical characteristics of objects and events—to describe and compare properties such as size, shape, hardness, color, and texture. Discovering the visible details of everyday objects becomes especially exciting when done with a homemade magnifier. Your child will better understand how lenses work by building one and be eager to use his or her own "invention."

How You Can Help

1. Using scissors or a pocket knife, cut three circles out of the sides of a plastic bucket. Each hole should be large enough for your child's hand to fit through.

2. Ask your child to cover the top of the bucket loosely with a sheet of plastic wrap, holding it in place with a rubber band or tape.

3. Have your child make a slight depression in the center of the plastic wrap and slowly pour water into it. The weight of the water will make the plastic sag into a convex shape resembling a lens. The more water your child adds, the more the plastic sags and the stronger the magnification.

4. Invite your child to place small objects inside the bucket. Ask him or her to observe and compare different physical properties such as size, shape, and color.

5. Invite your child to "optimize" the magnifier, trying different ways to improve the focus. Have him or her explore and test ideas without assistance, then offer some suggestions such as adjusting the plastic wrap, adding more water, raising or lowering the object, covering one of the side holes, or cutting more holes in the bucket.

Physical Science

Dear Parents,

Did You Know?

When your child takes apart and examines old machines, he or she strengthens critical-thinking skills. New technology often comes from "fine tuning" earlier discoveries. Researchers examine and experiment with old models to create new, improved versions. Help your child strengthen mechanical science skills by encouraging him or her to explore modern machines and how they operate.

How You Can Help

1. Provide your child with various cups (paper, plastic, Styrofoam), "connectors" (string, yarn, fishing line), large paper clips, tape, scissors, a tape measure, and a nail.

2. Ask your child to make a "phone line" using two Styrofoam cups and a ten-foot piece of string. Have your child use a nail to poke a small hole in the bottom of each cup. Ask him or her to thread the ends of the string through the holes, then secure the string in place by tying each end to a paper clip and placing tape over each hole.

3. Test the "telephones" with your child. With each person holding a cup, move apart from each other until the string is straight and taut. Have your child listen through the cup as you speak into yours.

4. Take turns speaking into and listening through the telephones. Test how well they work when you speak quickly, softly, or in a high voice, or a low voice. Have your child record the results.

5. Invite your child to make and test new, improved models using different supplies. Some variations may include using

   - paper or plastic cups.
   - smaller or larger cups.
   - different "connectors"—yarn or fishing line.
   - shorter or longer "connectors."

6. Encourage your child to read and discover how real telephones work. To extend learning, invite him or her to take apart and examine an old or broken telephone.

Dear Parents,

Did You Know?

Cooking popcorn is more than a tasty pastime—it's science in action! Helping your child discover how and why popcorn pops is a fun, hands-on approach to improving analytical and problem-solving skills. Use the following exploration to help your child unravel the mystery of popping corn and "pop" a little science into your home.

How You Can Help

1. Have your child count 1/4 cup of popcorn kernels. Ask him or her to count a second batch of kernels to match the first.

2. Ask your child to spread one batch in a single layer on a cookie sheet, then bake for 1-1/2 hours at 200°F.

3. While one batch is in the oven, help your child pop the other. Have him or her count popped and unpopped kernels, then record the results on paper.

4. Ask your child to measure with a ruler the length of different popped kernels. Have him or her find the average size by measuring ten separate kernels, adding the values together, and dividing the total by ten. Have your child write the answer on paper for future reference.

5. After 1-1/2 hours have passed (and you've enjoyed eating the first batch of popcorn), remove the baked kernels and let cool. Help your child pop this second batch using the same method as before. Have your child perform the same "tests"—comparing popped and unpopped kernels and finding the average size.

6. Invite your child to compare and discuss results from both tests. Ask your child questions such as *Which batch popped better? How do you know? Which kernels popped bigger? Why? Do you think canned corn would pop? Why or why not?*

7. After your child has given the matter some careful thought, explain and discuss the results. (When heated quickly, moisture inside a popcorn kernel turns to steam. The steam exerts pressure on the shell, eventually causing the kernel to burst open. Baked kernels do not pop as well because most of the internal moisture has been "cooked" out. Canned corn will not pop at all because the outer skin is not hard enough to trap moisture.)

Physical Science

Dear Parents,

Did You Know?

Children learn best when they see and experience science. They need to observe concrete examples and refer to related information in their "memory banks" before science concepts are fully understood. This is especially true when it comes to abstract concepts such as gravity—the invisible force that keeps us upright. The following activity will help your child see and experience the power and pull of gravity.

How You Can Help

1. Ask your child to stand with his or her heels against a wall, then place a dollar bill on the floor twelve inches from his or her feet. Challenge your child to pick up the money while keeping heels against the wall, and without moving his or her feet or bending his or her knees. (It can't be done!)

2. Have your child repeat the process, this time standing in the center of the room rather than against the wall. Can he or she pick up the dollar bill? Why?

3. Ask your child to sit in a straight-backed chair with his or her arms folded and feet flat on the ground. Challenge him or her to get up without leaning forward or using his or her hands. (It's impossible because the center of balance must be shifted forward in order to move.)

4. Have your child stand next to a wall so his or her left foot, hip, and shoulder are touching it. Invite your child to try lifting his or her right foot.

5. Discuss with your child how we keep our balance by shifting our body positions to establish our center of gravity. To illustrate this point, have your child stand in front of a full-length mirror, then lift one foot. Point out how his or her body moves in the opposite direction to reestablish the center of gravity to keep from falling over.

6. With this new piece of knowledge, have your child explain why picking up the money, getting out of the chair, and lifting his or her foot while leaning against the wall was impossible. (The wall and chair got in the way of being able to shift body positions and reestablish the center of gravity.)

Parent Letters for the Intermediate Grades ©1997 Creative Teaching Press

Dear Parents,

Did You Know?

Scientists are trained to notice small details, ones that may not be evident at first glance. Many important discoveries have been made because scientists were able to see and detect minute changes in substances and solutions. Help your child strengthen important science skills by encouraging him or her to "take another look." The following activity will help your child develop a "critical eye" for science.

How You Can Help

1. Cut out a magazine or newspaper picture containing lots of details, such as a busy street scene, a school yard, or an amusement park.

2. Invite your child to look at the picture for ten seconds, then turn it face down. Have him or her say aloud or draw on paper details about the picture. Discuss the results.

3. Invite your child to look at the picture for another ten seconds. This time, provide some strategies to work with, such as:

   - *Notice the color, shape, and size of different objects.*
   - *Mentally categorize what you see into groups, such as people, places, and things.*
   - *Look for any distinctive or unusual patterns.*
   - *Connect what you see to objects familiar to you. For example, a person in the picture may be wearing a jacket that reminds you of your own.*

4. After time is up, turn the picture face down again. Have your child explain or draw any additional details from memory.

5. Look at the picture together in depth. Have your child identify those details remembered accurately and those inaccurately recalled or missed altogether.

6. Discuss whether or not the strategies were helpful. Invite your child to think of other "memory strategies" to improve observation skills.

7. As a variation, invite your child to look at a picture for ten seconds, then answer questions about the picture from memory. For example, *What was the man carrying in his hand?*

8. Encourage your child to look for details and test his or her memory in other daily tasks such as remembering a grocery list or sharing details about a favorite film.

Parent Letters for the Intermediate Grades ©1997 Creative Teaching Press

Physical Science

Dear Parents,

Did You Know?

An important part of being a good scientist is keeping accurate records. Scientists use written records to learn from their mistakes and discover new ways to solve problems. Good record-keeping also allows future researchers to look back on what has been done and focus on new, unexplored areas of research. The following hands-on exploration shows your child how written records can be used to make "new and improved" discoveries.

How You Can Help

1. Use a screwdriver to make the hole in the top of a dish-soap bottle big enough to fit a small straw (coffee stirrer). Have your child make a bottle "launcher" by pushing 1/4 of the small straw into the bottle and securing the seal with clay.

2. Invite your child to make a "rocket" with a large straw (soda straw). Ask him or her to tape paper triangles on either side of the base and a paper "point" at the top. Have your child prepare the rocket for "blast off" by sliding it over the straw in the launcher.

3. Have your child prepare a "predictions and results" graph by labeling two columns on graph paper. Ask your child to predict how far the rocket will travel and record the guess on the graph.

4. Have your child squeeze the bottle to launch the rocket into the air. Ask him or her to measure the distance with a tape measure, then record and compare results to the prediction.

5. Invite your child to launch the rocket several more times, recording both predictions and results. Encourage your child to observe the rocket in motion, noting any possible problems with rocket parts.

6. Have your child compare predictions and results. Ask questions such as *Did your predictions improve? How do you know? How did the results help you make new predictions?*

7. Encourage your child to make new and improved rockets and/or launchers based on results from the first model.

Parent Letters for the Intermediate Grades ©1997 Creative Teaching Press

Dear Parents,

Did You Know?

Science is more meaningful when connected to real-life experiences. Children learn best when they see a purpose behind what they're learning. Help your child improve important science skills by connecting explorations and experiments to everyday events. The following hands-on activity shows your child the benefits of scientific discoveries.

How You Can Help

1. Divide the back of a metal cookie sheet into four columns. Cover the first column with sandpaper, leave the second column as is, wet the third, and place a layer of vegetable oil over the fourth.

2. Give your child a small, flat bottle. Have him or her predict what will happen when the bottle is slid down each column.

3. Hold the tray at an angle while your child lets the bottle slide down each column. Have him or her wipe the bottle before each test.

4. Discuss the results. Invite your child to explain why the bottle slides more easily on the wet, greasy surfaces than on the others. (Water and oil form a smooth layer between two surfaces which reduces friction.)

5. Discuss ways friction affects our everyday lives. Invite your child to give real-life examples of when frictionless surfaces are beneficial. For example, bowling alleys are polished to help balls travel easily, and oil is placed between moving machine parts to keep them operating smoothly.

6. Invite your child to give real-life examples of when frictionless surfaces are dangerous. For example, walking up a slippery hill, riding a bicycle on a rainy day, or driving a car when roads are icy.

7. Discuss ways we increase friction to avoid the dangers of slippery surfaces. For example, we make wheels with large treads, and spread gravel on icy roads.

Physical Science

Dear Parents,

Did You Know?

History is an ongoing adventure that involves reconstruction of the past. When children study history, they use critical-thinking skills to analyze and compare past and present events. One of the best ways to get your child interested in and enthusiastic about history is to start with his or her personal past. Use the following activity to help your child "travel back in time" to research and explore history in the making.

How You Can Help

1. Invite your child to make a Personal History Book using a blank journal from a bookstore or gift shop.

2. Have your child include a chapter for every year of his or her past. Include memories of people (relatives, friends, neighbors, classmates), places (homes, vacation spots, schools), and things (favorite toys, hobbies, awards, memorable and embarrassing moments).

3. Help your child get started by providing information such as

    *   when and where he or she was born.
    *   what other members of the family were doing on that day.
    *   what songs and movies were popular.

4. Invite your child to look through old photo albums. Share your memories of his or her childhood, and the excitement you felt during special moments such as birthdays, holidays, first words, first tooth, first day of school, and family trips.

5. Provide additional assistance by asking your child the following questions.

    *   *What is your first memory?*
    *   *Which favorite books and TV shows do you remember liking as a small child?*
    *   *What do you remember about our first home?*
    *   *What do you remember about your first best friend?*
    *   *What is your earliest memory about your brother(s) and/or sister(s)?*

6. Have your child include illustrations and photographs in his or her Personal History Book. Invite your child to share the book with family members and friends.

Parent Letters for the Intermediate Grades ©1997 Creative Teaching Press

Dear Parents,

Did You Know?

Many family experiences link directly to important historical events. When you awaken your child's curiosity about family history, you arouse interest in past worldwide incidents. Use the following activity to help your child discover family roots while experiencing oral and written history.

How You Can Help

1. Help your child construct a time line on his or her bedroom wall using adding-machine paper, shelf paper, or drawing paper.

2. Have your child draw a line across a long paper strip, then divide it into equal segments—one for each year of his or her life.

3. Ask your child to label each segment with the year, his or her age at that time, and an important family event. Invite your child to include illustrations and photographs.

4. Help your child supplement personal family events with important historical ones. Have your child search through library books, past newspapers, and old magazines to discover local or worldwide events that happened each year. Include the most intriguing information on the time line.

5. Invite older family members to share their memories of past events with your child. Encourage them to discuss childhood memories and how times have changed.

Dear Parents,

Did You Know?

You can teach your child history simply by reading aloud a good book! When children hear stories through folklore, myths, poetry, plays, biographies, and historical novels, they learn about "long-ago" people, places, and things. Classical literature is especially valuable for exploring and comparing changes in technology, clothing, family life, and beliefs. Help your child discover "historical perspective" by reading aloud a variety of exciting, captivating classics.

How You Can Help

1. Read together a book from a particular time period, such as *Little House on the Prairie* by Laura Ingalls Wilder or *Sherlock Holmes* by Sir Arthur Conan Doyle.

2. Compare the book's time period to present-day happenings. Discuss changes in transportation, clothing, housing, technology, schooling, family life, and general beliefs.

3. Have your child compare past and present cooking—the kinds of foods eaten, methods of obtaining food, and food preparation. For example, in *Little House on the Praire*, Laura's family churned their own butter, hunted for their meat, and cooked meals in a wood-burning stove.

4. Invite your child to prepare storybook foods. Encourage him or her to "dress the part" and serve food to family members.

5. Encourage your child to read and compare literature from other time periods. Make a chart or time line comparing similarities and differences.

Parent Letters for the Intermediate Grades ©1997 Creative Teaching Press

Dear Parents,

Did You Know?

History has more meaning for children when it relates to their immediate world. Make history fun and fascinating by sharing historical tidbits about familiar people and places. Try the following unique, gift-giving idea to help your child learn more about history while taking friends and relatives on a special trip down memory lane.

How You Can Help

1. Invite your child to give "historical" gift booklets to friends and relatives on their birthdays. Include facts and illustrations about the way the world was on that particular day.

2. Encourage your child to gather historical information by looking through old newspapers and magazines at the local library. Ask questions such as:

   - *What was happening in the news that day?*
   - *What was the weather like?*
   - *How have clothing styles changed?*
   - *How have food prices changed?*
   - *What kinds of machines and gadgets were available?*
   - *What songs and movies were popular?*

3. For added fun, invite your child to make 3-D booklets by including coins and trinkets from that time period.

Dear Parents,

Did You Know?

Everything that surrounds your child at home—chairs, dishes, books, toys—has a history. Exploring stories behind familiar items introduces your child to other times, expands his or her knowledge of your family ancestry, and provides opportunities to practice research skills. The following activity helps your child shift into "museum mode" by exploring objects and artifacts in and around the home.

How You Can Help

1. Have your child choose a favorite household object as a "museum piece." Have him or her imagine it is on display in a museum.

2. Help your child think of questions a museum visitor might ask about the object, such as:

    ● *Where did the object come from?*
    ● *How did the family acquire it and when?*
    ● *What was happening in our country and the world at that time?*

3. Discuss what your child already knows about the "museum piece." Invite him or her to ask you for additional facts.

4. Suggest that your child conduct interviews or send questionaires to older relatives to learn more about the object's history.

5. Encourage your child to learn more about the artifact's history by looking through reference books (e.g., an almanac) and talking to various professionals.

6. Extend learning by setting up a "then-and-now" display comparing old items to their modern counterparts. For example, a 78 RPM phonograph record to a CD, an old long-necked glass milk bottle to a milk carton, or a kerosene lantern to an electric lamp.

7. Invite your child to collect photographs and antique artifacts to create a "then-and-now" exhibit. Have your child write "historical-fact" cards to place with each display.

Parent Letters for the Intermediate Grades ©1997 Creative Teaching Press

Dear Parents,

Did You Know?

History of personal experiences has a lot more "staying power" than history of events alone. Although much of the personal side of history can't be found in textbooks, there are many children's books that do an excellent job making history "come to life." Whenever choosing books to read aloud with your child, look for stories that take place in the past.

How You Can Help

1. Read about an important historical figure such as a past president, humanitarian, explorer, or scientist.

2. Discuss with your child what it would be like to be that person and to actually live in that period of history. Ask your child questions such as:

   ● *What do you think would be the best thing about living then compared to today?*
   ● *How do you think your life would be different if you lived in that time period?*
   ● *What would you find worrisome, tedious, or scary about living in that time?*

3. Encourage your child to visit the local library to learn more about life during that time period.

4. One Saturday, invite your child to try a "time machine" exploration. Ask him or her to go through the day pretending to be the historical character living in the past. Have your child experience and perform daily routines—without the modern-day advantages!

5. Encourage your child to record in writing or on tape thoughts during the "time travel" experience. Invite your child to share the adventures with you and other family members.

6. Suggest that your child dress up as a historical character for Halloween. Encourage him or her to act the part, using a dramatic voice and sharing facts about the character's life.

Parent Letters for the Intermediate Grades ©1997 Creative Teaching Press

Dear Parents,

Did You Know?

Your child can learn history by watching old films. Motion pictures capture the essence of life and are a permanent record of days gone by. By viewing and comparing movies from different time periods, your child will better understand and appreciate the fads and trends carried over from generation to generation. Try the following interactive activities as your family watches history unravel in your own living room!

How You Can Help

1. Once a week, celebrate "oldies-but-goodies" night by watching and critiquing old movies. Select movies from different time periods, spanning from the 1920s to current times.

2. Have your child and other family members compare depicted trends and fads to current lifestyles. For example, compare and contrast clothing, hairstyles, language/slang, social interactions, cars and other motor vehicles, machines and technology (e.g., washing machines, televisions, computers), music, and dance.

3. Discuss what was happening in the world during the making of different movies. Explain how the tone of these films often reflected real-life feelings and emotions. For example, Shirley Temple movies were deliberately kept light and carefree to take people's minds off the troubles of World War Two.

4. Invite your child to make a "movie-history" chart with five columns—*Decade, Movie Title, Date Made, Noted Lifestyles,* and *Then and Now*. Have your child list decades in chronological order, beginning with 1920. Invite him or her to write observations about the movie under *Noted Lifestyles,* then compare these to current trends and fads under *Then and Now*.

Parent Letters for the Intermediate Grades ©1997 Creative Teaching Press

Dear Parents,

Did You Know?

Exploring maps not only helps children learn geography and history, but also provides opportunities to practice important math and problem-solving skills. Maps are especially appealing when used with games or interactive activities. Try the following real-life map activity the next time you invite company to your home. Your visitors will appreciate the directions, and your child will discover exciting new "pathways" to learning.

How You Can Help

1. Have your child draw a map that shows the best route to your home from a well-known crossroads or other location. Help your child choose a starting point that visitors will be able to find on their own.

2. Drive the family car slowly from that spot to your home. Ask your child to write down all important landmarks and turns along the route.

3. Have your child use the car's odometer to keep track of the mileage from one landmark or turn to another.

4. Once home, help your child put the information in map form. Ask your child to draw and label landmarks on the map. Use a ready-made map of the area to help your child locate north, south, east, and west on the homemade map. Use the mileage report to draw the map to scale. For example, if it's a ten-mile trip, one inch on the map could represent each mile.

5. Encourage your child to write directions to go with the map. Invite him or her to send copies to anyone traveling to your home.

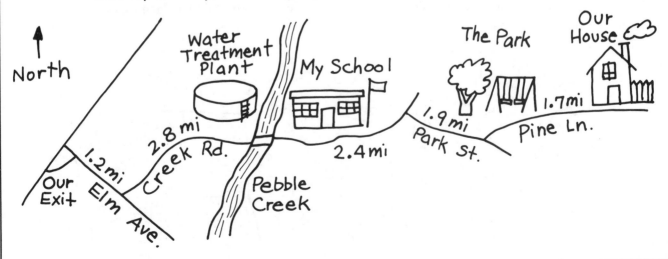

Dear Parents,

Did You Know?

Newspapers are excellent for motivating and encouraging children to learn geography. Children understand and appreciate the importance of geography when they see how it ties to real people and events. By skimming through newspapers or listening to you read articles aloud, your child learns meaningful information about people and places around the world. The next time you pull out the daily newspaper, try these "world-wide" activities with your child.

How You Can Help

1. Attach a large world map to a wall or bulletin board.

2. Have your child skim through the newspaper and cut out names of cities, states, and countries. Ask him or her to glue or pin them to the corresponding locations on the map. Invite your child to point to and identify rivers, lakes, oceans, and mountains surrounding these highlighted areas.

3. Invite your child to add the names of sports teams to different areas of the map. Place team names on their "home" cities or states. For added fun, invite your child to draw symbols to represent each sport, for example, a football, baseball, or soccer ball.

4. For further enrichment, invite your child to listen for names of cities and states in television news reports. Place star stickers on the map in the cities and states mentioned. Encourage your child to research and learn more about these news-worthy areas.

5. To extend learning, have your child copy the names of cities and states on paper strips. Cut the strips in half, mix them up, and invite your child to place matching pieces together.

Parent Letters for the Intermediate Grades ©1997 Creative Teaching Press

Dear Parents,

Did You Know?

With today's modern technology, you can help your child become a world traveler right in your own home! Televisions, video recorders, and computers are invaluable resources for teaching children geography. By watching news stories, international movies, and computer displays, your child can learn about international people, places, and things.

How You Can Help

1. Use a small blank booklet to make your child a "passport." Include a photograph of your child on the front page to make it "official."

2. Post local, country, and world maps on a bulletin board or wall.

3. Invite your child to keep a lookout for different places mentioned in television programs, videos, or computer software. (For example, countries mentioned in news stories or foreign films.)

4. Have your child locate and identify these regions on the maps, using pushpins or stickers.

5. Ask your child to write the names of these places in his or her passport, including one or more facts about each destination.

6. Challenge your child to "travel" to a number of destinations each week. Encourage him or her to research and discover more information about these foreign lands.

Geography

Dear Parents,

Did You Know?

Children are motivated to learn about geography and different cultures when they see objects and artifacts from around the world. When seeing items such as international stamps, toys, instruments, art, and clothing, children become curious about where the objects were made, how they are used, and the people who use them. Try the following unique, hands-on activity to bring "a piece of the world" into your home.

How You Can Help

1. Collect some first-class stamps, envelopes, index cards, a pen, a map of the United States, and a zip-code directory (available at post offices and libraries).

2. Ask your child to browse through the directory and make a list of names and addresses of places that catch his or her attention, for example, Loveland, Colorado; Boring, Maryland; and Kissimmee, Florida.

3. Invite your child to send a self-addressed, stamped envelope to the post office at each location, including a short note explaining that he or she is collecting postmarks. The postmaster will postmark the enclosed envelope and mail it back to your child.

4. Hang the map on a wall or large bulletin board. Once the postmarks arrive, have your child paste or pin the envelopes along the edges of the map, then draw lines or attach yarn pieces from the envelopes to the corresponding regions on the map.

5. Have your child supplement the collection by asking friends and relatives to mail him or her postcards when they travel.

6. To extend the activity, encourage your child to visit the local library and learn more about each location. Invite him or her to write "fascinating-fact" cards and pin them to the map along with the corresponding postmarks.

Parent Letters for the Intermediate Grades ©1997 Creative Teaching Press

Dear Parents,

Did You Know?

Children can learn to appreciate and understand different cultures by studying their own family history! Every family has ancestors that immigrated from one country to another. By exploring family heritage, your child is opening a whole new world of cultural experiences. Help your child become aware of family traditions, values, and beliefs as you build a family tree together.

How You Can Help

1. Purchase a large piece of poster board and colored construction paper.

2. Give your child a collection of old and new family photos. (You may choose to make color copies of the originals.) Discuss and share the history behind each picture. Include information about each person's birthplace and, if applicable, immigration to the United States.

3. Ask your child to place pictures in chronological order—oldest ancestor to most recent relative.

4. Invite your child to glue photos to construction-paper backings—a different color to represent each generation. For extra fun, have your child cut backings into different shapes such as ovals, squares, hearts, and stars.

5. Invite your child to make a family tree. Have him or her glue photos of the oldest ancestors in the center of the poster board, then branch out to more recent relatives. Draw lines (or glue yarn pieces) to show the connection between different generations.

6. Beneath each photo, have your child write the relative's name, date of birth, date of death (if applicable), birthplace, and relationship to your child.

7. To extend learning, invite your child to visit the local library to learn more about the birthplace of different ancestors. For extra enrichment, invite your child to write a family history book to go with the family tree.

Cultural Awareness

Dear Parents,

Did You Know?

Pictures and images are an important part of teaching cultural awareness. Children learn from both seeing and hearing about real people and places—words alone are not enough. Help your child understand and appreciate different cultures by sharing and discussing photographs of people from different countries. The following hands-on activity will help your child look more carefully and thoughtfully at the multitude of races and cultures in our world.

How You Can Help

1. Have your child cut out magazine and newspaper pictures of people from around the world.

2. Attach a world map to a wall or bulletin board.

3. Have your child glue or pin pictures around the map. Ask him or her to attach yarn pieces from the pictures to corresponding locations on the map.

4. Invite your child to look for photographs or draw illustrations depicting the culture of these people—clothing, housing, food, art, and religious celebrations. Glue or pin cultural portraits next to the people pictures.

5. To extend learning, invite your child to send care packages through the American Red Cross to countries in need.

Parent Letters for the Intermediate Grades ©1997 Creative Teaching Press

Dear Parents,

Did You Know?

Your child can learn about different cultures by playing with money! Foreign currency is an excellent way to motivate and teach children about distant lands. Children are fascinated by the colors and designs of foreign currency and are curious to learn more about it. By encouraging your child to examine and discuss various coins and bills, you not only strengthen math skills, but also develop an awareness of people and places from around the world. The following suggestions will help your child discover the "hidden value" of foreign currency.

How You Can Help

1. Collect real samples or photographs of foreign currency from around the world. (Check your local directory for foreign exchange brokers.)

2. Invite your child to examine and compare coins and bills.

3. Use current exchange rates (see your local newspaper) to help your child calculate the U.S. equivalence of foreign currency. For example, 125 Spanish pesetas equals one American dollar.

4. Encourage your child to research and discover the cost of living in various countries. Look through travel booklets or ask for price listings from local travel agents.

5. Invite your child to learn more about people and places pictured on coins and bills. Have him or her identify who or what is pictured, what the person or structure is famous for, and when the individual lived or the structure was built.

6. To extend learning, have your child make a "currency-and-culture" book. Glue or tape a coin or bill to each page, then write facts about the country from which the currency originates.

Cultural Awareness

Dear Parents,

Did You Know?

People from different cultures often portray their feelings, beliefs, and customs through literature, music, art, and cooking. Help your child understand and appreciate other cultures by exploring poems, plays, crafts, songs, dances, and foods from around the world. Try the following "tasty" activity to help your child become a cultural connoisseur.

How You Can Help

1. Invite your child to look through books, magazines, and newspapers to find international recipes to try at home.

2. Celebrate International Meal Day once a week. Invite your child to help prepare foods from around the world. For example, one week prepare and serve Spanish food, the next week Irish food, and so on.

3. Before International Meal Day, encourage your child and other family members to read about the country being "celebrated." At meal time, take turns sharing interesting or unusual facts you've learned.

4. Point out the country's location on a world map. Tie in map activities such as finding

    ● travel distance from your home to the country.
    ● names of surrounding countries.
    ● the direction to travel (north, south, east, or west) from your home state to the country.
    ● time zones.

5. Invite your child to make a cookbook of favorite international recipes. Add "spice" to the book by including illustrations, photographs, and interesting facts about the countries from which recipes originated.

Parent Letters for the Intermediate Grades ©1997 Creative Teaching Press